EMPATHY

The Art of Effective Chaplaincy:
A Companion in the Darkness

MICHAEL TURNER

EMPATHY

Acknowledgements

To my wife, Yvonne, whose support and love has been a constant in my life since we met. I love you.

To Cathy Gault and Rev. Jonathan Boyle for having the courage, love and respect for patients that they reflected on the training in pastoral care, and then improved it out of this world.

Personal friends and relatives were very helpful as well: especially Rocky Biasi and Veronica Gaweda. God bless you all.

Last but not least, I dedicate this small work to God, who like a loving attentive Parent, calls unworthy persons into His service, as His representative as chaplains, in order to remind His children in crisis that heaven is not deaf, and that God has not forgotten them in the "valley of the shadow of death".

Table of Contents

Foreword

By Rocky Biasi

I've known Michael Turner for 45 years. That's not the only reason I'm honoured to write the forward to this transformational book.

In my experience as a teacher, school counsellor and also in private practice for 25 years I've witnessed the often well intentioned responses to people in distress that create more harm than good. In 2008 I decided to create a training programme (The Accidental Counsellor) to help people listen and respond to emotional distress without burning out.

Michael and I are both trained as counsellors, however when Michael started in his role as a chaplain in a major Sydney hospital, he was introduced to a different way of BEING with a person in distress – what he calls the *Pastoral Conversation*.

I still recall his many experiences and examples of applying the new skills of a pastoral conversation and marvelled at the remarkable transformation people experienced as a result. If you're wondering what are these skills? Is it some type of amazing advice or questioning techniques that help people in distress? The clear and overwhelming answer is NO!

The work of a counsellor is to help people make changes in their lives. This is often misunderstood as if the counsellor has the answer and the skills to help the person make changes.

This misunderstanding is often expressed as, "So what did the counsellor say"? This is very different to being with someone in a pastoral conversation. What both approaches have in common is that people have their own resources and agency, strengths and solutions that are best suited for themselves.

Our role in helping people access these inner resources is to create a safe loving space where the person feels heard and listened to, acknowledged and validated. In this environment a person who is emotionally distressed no longer feels alone. It's like they are in a dark pit and when you arrive with this ability to not project your own triggers and agenda but rather listen to what's said and unsaid and respond in a way that makes the person feel you "get it" or at least trying to get it - well the result can be transformative.

I highly recommend this book and will share it with everyone in my audience who seeks to support others in emotional distress.

Rocky Biasi

Introduction

Having a connection with others is really what makes life worth living. Who among us enjoys feeling isolated and lonely? Sure, some alone time is important, but as I reflect on my life, the most wonderful times have been with others. For many decades I have had an interest in developing skills in which building connection with others was the focus, and to that end I read books, completed courses, and sought to practice what I had learnt. I knew that all of us desired connections with others, and understood the importance of such, not only in our social and personal lives, but also within our working lives. I thought that I was a person who had reached a high level of communicating with others and had the ability to use empathy in order to build those connections. However, it wasn't until I began my work as a hospital chaplain, that I was introduced to a method of communicating, called a pastoral conversation, that I realised just how effective empathy was in building connection with others, and that I could build that connection quickly.

The most significant person to impact on my effectiveness as a chaplain was Cathy Gault. Cathy was the Manager of the Pastoral Care Department at Nepean Hospital, a 520-bed teaching hospital and regional trauma centre, providing tertiary referral services for the Nepean Blue Mountains Local Health District. Cathy had taken a chance on a me, a new chaplain who had no chaplaincy experience, but in whom she saw an 'empty cup' and she hoped I would be willing to practice the skills necessary to make me an effective chaplain in the hospital. I often teased Cathy that she was the President of the Stephen Covey Fan Club, because she often quoted his many valuable insights. One of Cathy's favourite Covey saying was: "Begin with the end in mind", or as Cathy personalised it: What's your end in mind?

So, as I begin this unpacking of the training developed by Cathy and Jonathan, this question comes to mind. The answer: my end in mind is to offer to others the opportunity to learn a very effective method of building a connection quickly with others; the skills necessary to engage in an empathic conversation; and thereby improving every relationship you have. For myself, I learnt this method of using empathy in order to connect quickly with patients in a hospital environment, but I soon realised that this method of conversing, which I found so fruitful in my work, also began to change my personal relationships.

I see clearly now how different a chaplain I would have been if I'd never had this training. Believing I was already skilled enough to engage with another, I would never have known just how much was missing from my potential. You don't know what you don't know! The training that I committed to learn, and which has shaped so much of what I do as a chaplain, is now yours to engage with and practice. What should be clear, is that this transformation within yourself, as well as acquiring the skills necessary to build connection quickly with others, is up to you. This book is but the starting point. What you do with the information contained is up to you. It's surprising how much of a chaplain's role is about preparing the chaplain themselves.

For my part, I would encourage you to practice the contents of this book, even if like me originally, you think so much of it seems counter-intuitive. If you practice the skills within this book, and work on becoming comfortable in the 'darkness', especially your own, then the fruits of this training will become obvious and a shift in both you and the Other will begin to occur. Enjoy the journey. I assure you it's worth it.

The Miracle of the Loaves and Fishes is a biblical passage which I can relate to my ministry as a hospital chaplain. I include the version from St. Matthew's Gospel 14: 13-21: -

*Now when Jesus heard this, he withdrew from there in a boat to a lonely place apart. But when the crowds heard it, they followed him on foot from the towns. As he went ashore, he saw a great throng; and he had compassion on them and healed their sick. When it was evening, the disciples came to him and said, "This is a lonely place, and the day is now over; send the crowds away to go into the villages and buy food for themselves." Jesus said, "They need not go away; **you give them something to eat**."*

They said to him, "We have only five loaves here and two fish." And he said, "Bring them here to me."

Then he ordered the crowds to sit down on the grass; and taking the five loaves and the two fish he looked up to heaven, and blessed, and broke and gave the loaves to the disciples, and the disciples gave them to the crowds. And they all ate and were satisfied. And they took up twelve baskets full of the broken pieces left over. And those who ate were about five thousand men, besides women and children.

This very special gospel event speaks to me in a strong way of the ministry of hospital chaplains. The hospital I work at has over 500 beds and includes Mental Health wards. There is only a small team of chaplains, and the "great throng" is always present. Sometimes the difference between those two numbers can seem overwhelming. However, our Lord challenges me, "You give them something to eat". I answer, "Lord, there are too many, it's beyond my ability". The Lord then takes my *'five loaves and two fish'* and works a miracle every day. Each day, a small team of chaplains, venture forth into the wards to meet so many who are struggling and in crisis, and through the little we have to offer them, God's love makes up for what is lacking, often in abundance.

sweet darkness by david whyte

When your eyes are tired,

the world is tired also. When your vision has gone,

no part of the world can find you.

Time to go into the dark

where the night has eyes

to recognize its own.

There you can be sure

you are not beyond love.

The dark will be your womb

tonight.

The night will give you a horizon

further than you can see.

You must learn one thing:

the world was made to be free in.

Give up all the other worlds

except the one to which you belong.

Sometimes it takes darkness and the sweet

confinement of your aloneness

to learn

anything or anyone

that does not bring you alive

is too small for you.

Chapter One

Social Conversation and Pastoral Conversation

"In the middle of the journey of our life I found myself within a dark wood where the straightway was lost." ...

Dante's Inferno

I vividly remember my first day as the new chaplain. I still didn't have much of a clue as to what I would be doing. Sure, I had the big picture: that is, I would visit assigned wards in order to engage with patients. That much I got. There are of course other duties of a hospital chaplain, but visiting patients formed the bulk of what I was to do. I was to discover, that my initial tasks were to learn (1) What is a pastoral conversation (PC), (2) what were the elements of the pastoral conversation and (3) to be able recognise how it differed from a social conversation, and then (4) practice containing the elements of a social conversation when engaged in a pastoral conversation.

A pastoral conversation is a conversation in which a person shares something which is meaningful and contains emotion and loss. It differs from someone sharing, for example, about their love of roses, or their coin collection, which would be more of a social conversation. It also differs from what I would call a 'moan', in which a person lists their sufferings, but in a matter-of-fact way, without any emotional input. We have all met people who seem more than ready to share a litany of issues and tragedies to anyone and everyone who is willing to listen. It appears to be their strategy for eliciting sympathy and attention from others. That's not what I am talking about.

A pastoral conversation often emerges after some time engaging in a social interaction, when for some reason a person feels they can share something very personal and often something they didn't intend too. Many times, I have heard people say, "I don't know why I shared that with you. I had no intention when you sat down, of bringing that up". There are times when a person will just share their sufferings as soon as the conversation starts, as if they had been desperately waiting for someone to arrive with the promise of a 'listening' ear, but this seems the exception rather than the rule. Often people will 'test' us out by sharing something much safer and more 'respectable', before deciding if they want to mention their ultimate concern/s to us. One of the key features of our role is we don't have any responsibility for the direct care of the patient, and therefore, we can be a flexible, neutral party with whom a patient can share concerns, fears or any other emotion. A chaplain could be whatever the patient needed, even if that was a person to scream at and throw out of the room.

Having undertaken counselling training courses, I felt I already possessed the necessary skills needed to have a pastoral conversation with someone, but this was before I understood what a 'pastoral' conversation was. However, as I began to learn the various elements of the PC, I started to realise how different it was from what I had been doing, and what I thought or expected would be my role as a hospital chaplain. I also realised, that this method was an incredibly useful starting point for people such as counsellors. This method would enable them to build connection quickly, and then using the rapport which they had developed, be able to guide those they were engaged with more easily.

I thought my role would essentially be like a walking dispenser of hope. I would visit those who were in crisis or feeling hopeless, and by the time I left, hope would have been restored. I came to see that ultimately this was true in many instances, but the restoration of hope came from the patient themselves, not me.

When I think about the patients in the hospital, I imagine that they are all to some degree in a 'pit', in other words, they are undergoing a time of crisis. The depth of these 'pits' are as different as each person is different but, I visualise that each patient is in their own 'pit'. At times the 'content' of the 'pit' has to do with the present, sometimes the past, and sometimes both; but it is a space containing very strong emotions and significant loss. It's what I have called the 'darkness'. Humans instinctively don't like the darkness, we prefer the light, and with our own dark inner world it's the same. We all have a variety of ways of avoiding our 'darkness' (wherein lies all our wounds/hurts/betrayals/ grief/loss etc.), ways of practicing a type of conscious forgetfulness in order to not to have to look at that place within us. However, there are times and occasions when we either choose to look into our 'pit' or we fall in, and we can become afraid, sad, or angry.

When I visit patients, the only agenda I have is to create a space where a person feels free to share anything they like, and my willingness to accompany them wherever they may lead. Often a conversation starts on the social level, and I would simply 'follow' wherever the person would lead. If our sharing stayed on the social level, that was fine, but if the conversation shifted to a deeper more personal level, then I would follow as well. I do not force my way into someone's 'pit' or try and drag them down there. I listen for a shift in the conversation, from social to pastoral, and this shift would indicate the 'invitation' to join them in their darkness. When the conversation shifts, I shift. For example, a patient may say, "The most beautiful thing in the world was my roses, but after the death of my husband, it seemed like all the beauty in the world vanished". In this example, the patient and I may have been sharing our thoughts on roses, but when the conversation shifts to the loss of her husband, then I shift. I no longer keep talking about plants, and for that time, the social conversation is over, and the pastoral conversation begins. This 'shift' is completely controlled by the patient, who chooses to change the topic from roses to the death of her husband. My task is to follow her into the 'pit' and to listen, with intention and attention, to what is said directly, and what may be the message behind the message, to observe clues in their body language, and then feedback responses that indicate a level of understanding. When and if she changes the conversation back to social, then I follow as well.

My goal is not to keep the person any longer in the 'pit' than they want. I have had patients 'dip their toe' into their 'darkness' with one single meaningful comment, only to have them withdraw back to the safety of the social conversation. That's fine. I allow the person the space and time they need. Perhaps the next visit or the next chaplain will be 'invited' for a longer stay in their 'pit', but it's not up to me to push them to stay in their pain. It must come from them. Whilst I mentioned that the 'shift' was completely up to the patient, that is not entirely true, because I can do a lot as a chaplain to create a space, an atmosphere, where the other person feels like this could be the time to unload a weight on their heart. I can also sabotage any attempt by the other person to *drag me* into their pit. However, if I am following this training, then an opportunity is created, and then it is completely up to the patient, and I just follow their lead.

This is where any negative, un-faced emotional triggers I have, could interfere with the process. This is where a chaplain may be tempted to say, "I know it's hard to lose your husband, but you know he wouldn't like to see you sitting around so sad. What other things do you like to do besides your gardening?" This response comes from a chaplain who has not done their own inner work on their 'dark' emotional triggers and wants to avoid the painful memories they have of their own losses. Grundmann (2003, p.3) notes that giving quick answers like this is actually a subtle means of "*not really getting exposed to the situation*", and this is what chaplains may unconsciously do when they have not done this inner work that allows them to comfortably sit in the 'darkness': their own or another's.

So, there are these two very distinct types of conversations, and it's essential for the chaplain to know the difference between the two and be equally comfortable with both. Like two separate languages, a chaplain must be fluent in both. We all come with a fair degree of proficiency in the social conversation, but the pastoral conversation is more elegant and difficult to master.

As a result of patterns of communication that we adopt from society and culture, we all learn to engage with each other in a certain way, and that manner of engaging may never be questioned. Most of the time, people are unaware how asking questions, or offering advice/solutions, or sharing similar stories of woe, can prevent a deeper connection from occurring. We often think it's the opposite, i.e., if I share with the person that I have been through something similar, then they will feel I understand what they are going through. Instead, don't share your experience, but draw on the memory of how it felt so as you can feedback to the person what it might be like for them. This helps keep the focus on the other person and not us. In this way, the pastoral conversation requires a degree of forgetfulness: forget the normal way you converse, because the pastoral conversation is quite different from our normal social conversing.

Before even beginning any further clarification between these two types of conversation, let me stress me how important it is that patients be offered the *choice* about whether they wanted to speak with us or not.

Our Introduction to the encounter.

When we visit patients, we need to be respectful of the fact that some patients will not want a visit from us. I like to imagine that a patient in their hospital bed is like a person sitting in their living room: you don't just walk into somebody's living room uninvited and start talking. We must offer the person a chance to say, "No thanks" to our visit. Often, tired out emotionally and physically, patients may long just to be left alone, and this is why a choice must be given as to whether they want to engage with us or not.

I remember seeing a chaplain walk into a patient's room, spot some photos of what they assumed were the grandchildren on the table beside the bed, and straight away said, "Oh, are they your grandchildren? They're beautiful. What's their names?" The patient was trying to process who this person was walking into their hospital room and wondering where they fit in as part of the health team. They sheepishly answered, looking a bit annoyed. The chaplain then introduced herself and asked further questions about the grandkids. There is no choice offered here, just an intrusive chaplain. This is disrespectful and gives chaplains a 'bad name'. Most people are too polite to shut a chaplain like this down and they tolerate this intrusion until the chaplain decides they have had enough and leave.

We must introduce ourselves and give this respectful choice to people. I have seen new chaplains really grapple with getting the introduction right, and it does take some time and thought to make your introduction your own. Essentially it must clearly describe who you are, and why you are there, and come with a choice, for example,

"Hello, my name is Michael. I am one of the hospital chaplains, and I am visiting the ward today to see if anyone would like a visit. Is this something you would like"?

Now in this increasingly secular society, more and more people are unsure what a 'chaplain' is, but at least here in Australia, it tends to carry the idea that this person is 'religious' and usually are representing one of the many denominations that exist. Many times, a patient will respond, "Oh I'm not religious", so the patient understands that the chaplain is religious, and they think therefore that we won't want to speak with them if they're not. It's like a family member or friend approaching us and saying, "I've joined Amway. Can I come around and share some of their wonderful products?" We just imagine we are going to get the 'hard sell' even if that is not the intention of the new Amway member. Our patients just imagine that as the chaplain, we are going to do something *'religious*, like preach or ascertain if they have given their life to the Lord. At times, the patient may still be processing the word 'chaplain' before they realise that I am *not* a member of the health team in the traditional sense. At these times, a patient who politely just answered "Yes" to my offer, may then realise in horror that they have asked a 'religious-freak' to sit down and may wonder how to get rid of me. There are clear sign that a person did not really want me to sit down after all, and these typically include (1) when I sit down, they ask, "What do you want to talk about?" like they are doing you a favour, or (2) two or three minutes into the conversation they start asking me questions about myself. In these cases, I will politely get the hint, answer a couple of questions about me, and then "Thank" them for their time and move on. I don't give up immediately, for example, if they ask me, "What do you want to talk about?", I might respond, "Why don't you tell me what's most important to you right now?" or, "What are you most passionate about?", or "What's the worst part of this for you?" Depending on how these questions are answered determines the likely amount of time I will be with that person. I have had some wonderfully deep and dark 'pit' encounters through the use of these questions at the very start of an encounter.

Work on your own introduction, but make sure it has all the necessary ingredients. I would add, that if a patient wants to engage with you, then sit down, and don't stay standing. I will look for a chair, or even go and get one from another room. Not only does this ensure I'm more physically comfortable, which will be an obvious aid to listening, but it gets me down to their eye level, or close to it.

Elements of the Social Conversation

The next step in the process begins by outlining the differences between a social and pastoral conversation. I will begin with the elements of the social conversation which I'm sure everybody will recognise:

- Mutual sharing of stories & thoughts regarding a variety of topics, for example, -personal news about family,
  - -Church, or work life,

- ○ -General interest topics such as the weather, local or overseas news, sport etc.
- Curiosity expressed as an interest in the other person, i.e., lots of questions.
- The maintaining of a congenial atmosphere is a priority. Nothing too deep and meaningful. Light topics typically.
- Best if pleasant, positive, humorous, and entertaining. Avoid Silences.
- Different opinions discussed, as long as it doesn't get too heated
- Often going off on tangents
- Advice offered and given.

This was straightforward enough, of course, although I was wondering what was going to be a problem with asking questions in a pastoral conversation or sharing of similar stories? In my long and winding road to chaplaincy, I had spent time in the NSW Police Force and also, in my counselling studies, I had found the asking of questions to be a useful tool, not only to gather more information about a situation in order to understand better what was going on, but it also conveyed the idea that I was interested in the situation or the story I was listening too.

I recall in the beginning, that not asking questions in a pastoral conversation was my biggest challenge, and the main reason I was not receiving the 'invitation' to enter the patient's 'pit'. It took me some time to realise just how asking questions prevented what I was trying to do.

Elements of the Pastoral Conversation

A chaplain has a variety of tasks in the hospital but engaging in conversations with patients/staff/and visitors remains the bulk of what we do, and so understanding the difference in these two very different types of conversations was essential.

Elements of the pastoral conversation:

- The focus is on the other
- Control your curiosity, minimal if any questions needed
- Accepts tension areas
- Comforts through facing issues
- Helps the person share himself/herself through the use of empathy to convey understanding or attempting to understand the other
- Being specific: what they/you do think, feel
- Non argumentative, especially in areas of religion
- Offer more than a "Sorry".
- Avoid offering advice
- No fixes or solutions. Don't put silver linings on situations
- The other controls the direction of the conversation
- Active, attentive silence

Miriam Berkowitz (2018) offers an excellent summary of the pastoral conversation, stating:

The main gift of pastoral care is a fully attentive, interested, respectful witness to each person's story and a gentle presence who allows people to speak things they have held inside for years, take control, express their needs, and connect with the highest aspects of themselves and the Divine. Chaplains look behind external labels and engage with each person's unique combination of personal history, world view, culture, personality and spiritual needs.

I came into chaplaincy believing I was already skilled in the art of conversing with people, and therefore at first, I didn't put into practice what I was being taught. I just went to the ward and continued in the same manner I always had when speaking with someone. The thing was, I had been told that when I began to practice the elements of the PC, and at the same time contain the elements of a social conversation, I would notice a shift in the type of conversation I was having. Simply put, by utilising the above elements of the PC, rapport could be built quickly, and the invitation to join them in their 'pit' could also follow promptly. This, of course, would reduce the number of social, chit-chat, coffee-shop type of conversation that a person could have with anyone and increase the probability of having a more meaningful encounter with the other. As a result of my inability to trust the elements of the PC, the first few weeks in my new role were exhausting. I noticed that engaging in social conversations (whilst not unimportant to the other) was draining for me. It is true that in this time, patients offered me a chance to enter their 'pit', but by asking questions and being curious, I unwittingly sabotaged their efforts to have me connect with them. After four weeks I realised I was not enjoying going through the hospital having social conversations with patients. It was at this point that I decided I needed to put into practice the training I had been receiving but not utilising. What I was at least doing, was reflecting on my experience, and this was telling me something was wrong with my approach. As anyone will attest, changing one's pattern of unconscious behaviour is not easy. However, I was determined to achieve this, or else face the prospect of a short-lived ministry as a chaplain.

I soon noticed the shift I had been told about. I was starting to have conversations where patients were revealing tragedies, and other very personal experiences of loss, grief, betrayal and abuse. The interesting aspect for me, was this belaying into one 'pit' after another had an energising effect. I was no longer feeling drained, bored, or essentially, useless. The pastoral conversation allows for a 'space' which is characterised by a deep, respectful, non-judgmental listening combined with empathic responses. In this 'space' I was seeing at one end of the spectrum that people were comforted, but at the other end, I was seeing these grand transformations: people looked younger, renewed, re-vitalised. Empathy and being understood were powerful transformers for people, and it showed me how rare this type of conversing was in people's experience and how eager they were to be listened to in this manner. I began to look forward to going to work and being that "instrument of peace" that St. Francis of Assisi spoke of in his powerful prayer:

Lord, make me an instrument of your peace:

where there is hatred, let me sow love;

where there is injury, pardon;

where there is doubt, faith;

where there is despair, hope;

where there is darkness, light;

where there is sadness, joy.

O divine Master, grant that I may not so much seek

to be consoled as to console,

to be understood as to understand,

to be loved as to love.

For it is in giving that we receive,

it is in pardoning that we are pardoned,

and it is in dying that we are born to eternal life.

Amen.

Old patterns do not change quickly or easily (typically at least), and I was working hard at moving from being *unconsciously incompetent* to being *consciously incompetent*. Knowing what the path is and taking it can be two very separate things. This is where step (4) comes in: practice. For me it was slow going, but over time and with determination, I moved toward being *consciously competent*, and to this day I'm working towards being *unconsciously competent*.

I will concentrate on exploring the elements of the PC, because as I have mentioned, for example, the *asking of questions* seemed to be misplaced as an essential or near-essential requirement. There are elements of course which are quite apparent (at least I think), so I will go through the elements which are not obvious.

(i) Asking questions:

As a result of my social conditioning, my counselling studies, and my time in the NSW Police Force, the asking of questions came as naturally to me as breathing. For the life of me I couldn't see what was wrong with that. It conveyed both interest and a desire for a greater grasp of the story. What I discovered was the asking of questions was not only unnecessary in a PC but keeps both persons from the 'pit'. In a later section, *Managing Triggers,* I will not only outline the benefits for managing these powerful emotions that can so easily sabotage an encounter, but how *not* managing our triggers for various reasons (usually fear and discomfort) act like the asking of questions: they keep us from entering the darkness of the 'pit'.

I want to share an interaction with a patient I visited very early after starting to practice the PC. I had been asked to see a young man, who had been taken to one of the post-surgical wards after being in ICU for several weeks. This man in his early 20's had, just a few weeks before I met him, played in a soccer Grand Final, which his team had won. After the match, he noticed that his thigh was quite sore, although he could not remember being struck on his thigh in any manner that would account for this discomfort. This young man went on to tell me, that the discomfort grew worse, and that the next day he was in ICU, and it was not certain at all if he would survive. He then went on to share with me that he now faced the prospect of 12 months rehabilitation, the loss of his employment, the loss of the family home, the loss of his active everyday life with his wife and three young kids. He was concerned how all this stress was going to affect his marriage, including the loss of intimacy that was normal in their young marriage. He was concerned about the costs of travelling to and from the hospital for his wife, the parking costs and the dragging of three young kids with her each day to see her husband. Plus, the prospect that this was going to be a lasting issue for the foreseeable future. Couple with this was the possibility of a lasting disability in which he would be unable to walk again without the aid of a device. This was as deep and dark a 'pit' as I had been into, and I was triggered.

A part of me desperately wanted to ask him, "What the heck happened?" I wanted to know, not only out of natural curiosity, but I wanted to avoid any chance this might happen to me. I did not ask. I contained my curiosity. I listened, tried to imagine what this must be like for him (asking myself, "What would I possibly feel if I was in this situation?), and feeding that back to him, in an attempt to show some attempt at understanding. He shared with me that it had helped. He told me that I had done what no one else had yet done: listened, emphasised, and not offer some cheap fix or platitude. I was following the PC training, and it provided a level of comfort and understanding he received from no one else. He called me three or four times over the next couple of months when he needed to be in a space where there was zero notion of fixing or offering some silver-lining to the situation. He just needed to be heard without any attempt to rescue or fix. Due to his fitness and youth, he did progress quickly and was moved to a specialist rehabilitation clinic sooner than he imagined, and he appeared on my office doorstep eight months later having made a full recovery. I still remember returning to the Pastoral Care Department after this encounter and doing two things: (1) announcing that I resisted asking any questions with considerable pride; and (2) looking up information on what I came to discover was Compartment Thigh Syndrome. I realised that in every PC I had, the asking of questions was typically unnecessary and would have been more about some need or curiosity of mine, rather than the need of the other person.

B. Preston Bogia, in his article, *Responding to Questions in Pastoral Care,* states that questions asked by the chaplain can be experienced as attacks, intrusions or demand. Typically, questions do demand an answer, and in this way can put people on the defensive, especially 'Why' questions. The problem is we have all been taught that it is not considered polite to ignore questions, and so we feel we must provide an answer. Once more it must be emphasised that questions in a social context and their use in a pastoral conversation is vastly different. There seems to be a superficiality about questions asked in a social setting, as they are not usually personal and often deal with matters of general knowledge.

Questions from the chaplain are seen as different. The questions from the chaplain may come from a loving heart, with pure intentions, however, the effect is to put the other on the defensive. It seems often the case, that when we feel stuck in a conversation or unsure what to say next, we may fall back on asking questions, but there are alternatives. Using statements rather than questions, especially if done skilfully, can be a better way to elicit information and at the same time, encourages elaboration. Borgia notes that stating an observation about a physical fact, such as, "There are tears in your eyes" can elicit a response that would be more 'telling' than the question, "Why are you crying?"

The use of sounds and grunts can be very useful in filling these spaces in a PC with someone. Such sounds as, "Oh", "Mm-hm", "Hmmm" and "Uh-huh" serve a chaplain well when conversing as it also allows the person to continue with what they are sharing with me, with only a second or two taken to convey clearly, "I'm with you". In the following section on the use of the word 'Sorry', I discuss that we need to be more elegant in the words we use, but that does not mean that there are times when these sounds/grunts can convey so much to the person we are listening to.

Borgia goes on to note that questions asked by the patient are almost always intended to convey a message. We are so used to asking questions that at first, we may not fully grasp what Borgia means when he says that questions convey a message, but this fact is noticeable to anyone paying attention. For example, if I ask my son where he is going as he heads toward the front door, I may not care about his destination, but I may care that his chores are not done. So, the meaning is, "Stop, and explain why your chores are not done, and yet you seem to be going out?" The point is that questions can be statements and can be heard as such with practice.

(ii) Offer more than a 'Sorry'

In our culture, saying "Sorry" comes so naturally, it can be hard to stop using that word. I am certain that most people know what we mean when we say 'Sorry', i.e.

I wish that you didn't have to go through what you are going through.

One only has to watch any TV show or movie, to hear just how many times the word 'Sorry' is used as a way of stating how we feel in response to another's situation. Of course, some people when you respond with "I am so sorry" will respond, "Why? It's not your fault". Indicating, that to that person, your "Sorry" is unnecessary and misplaced. I remember when I had left my last employment before starting as a chaplain, the State Manager of my training company offered to drive me home, as I no longer had a work vehicle. On the way home, he shared with me how his wife had recently been diagnosed with terminal cancer. I responded, "Alan, I am so sorry that this has happened to you both". He responded, "Oh, I didn't want to upset you, I shoulda (sic) kept my mouth shut". In this instance, Alan took my response of "Sorry" as meaning this was hard for me to hear and perhaps upsetting for me. It was a valuable lesson I recalled when I was tempted to offer a 'Sorry" to patients, and knew I had to do better and be clearer in what I was trying to say.

I want to challenge chaplains, as people whose main task is engaging in conversation, to be more thoughtful in your responses. Word choice matters. I want to challenge you to do more, offer more, come-up with more than a simple, "I'm sorry". I think we owe the other person a more elegant, thoughtful response to their circumstances.

I remember when I was in the process of completing one of my Clinical Pastoral Education courses, and in the group of facilitators and students, I raised this issue. We had just worked through a verbatim from one of the students in which he used the phrase, "I'm sorry" many times. So, when it came time to give feedback to the student, nobody else mentioned the over-use of this phrase, and so I offered it to the group for reflection and comment. I was met with total resistance. My perspective on this over-used phrase was not 'held' by the group for even a moment. Every member of the group provided me with an instance in which they had used that phrase, and "It worked perfectly". I was surprised with the level of opposition to what I was saying, and it felt like I was trashing some sacred dogma. After this session, whilst making a coffee in the small tearoom, I bumped into one of the facilitators, and I said, "Oh, I'm sorry". He responded, "Oh, you will say "Sorry"? with a sarcastic smile on his face. I responded, "I have no problem apologising if I bump into someone by accident, but I believe in a pastoral conversation, in the face of someone's suffering, we can do better than try and get away with the use of that phrase".

The following week, one of the students announced, "During the week my Mother-in-law passed away. But she was more of a mother than a mother-in-law". Each person in the group took turns saying, "Sorry for your loss". I said to him, "How devastating to lose such an important person from your life. Truly a heartbreaking and irreplaceable wound to your heart. Your life will never be the same again". He looked at me, and said, "Thanks for understanding what she meant to me".

On the first day of the most recent training course I ran for new hospital volunteer chaplains, I was sharing with the group how I think we need to do better than just say "Sorry" to the people we meet in the hospital. At morning tea, one of my students told me they realised that being a hospital volunteer was not for them, and that they were withdrawing from the course. I heard later that this same student had simply applied to another hospital to be a volunteer chaplain, and when asked why he had left my training, he responded, "I'm not going to be told what I can and cannot say. Ridiculous! What's wrong with saying 'Sorry'?

Saying, "I'm sorry" is about me, it's not about you. I'm telling you how I feel, what my response is to your sorrow and suffering. As a chaplain, I want my responses to be about you. I'm not suggesting that saying 'Sorry' to someone in a pastoral conversation should be a capital offense, but I would ask chaplains to work hard at dropping this phrase from your pastoral care vocabulary. There may be times when this phrase just 'pops' out because we are so used to its use, but then simply recognise it, and decide again to be more mindful and thoughtful, as to be better at communicating understanding and empathy to the other.

(iii) <u>No fixes, advice or solutions. Don't put silver linings on situations.</u>

By far, the biggest challenge I have seen with other chaplains, volunteers and student chaplains, along with virtually everybody else as well, is the difficulty of not offering fixes/solutions/ advice/ or platitudes to those we meet in crisis. It seems like we have all been trained to just want to make the other person feel better or help them see a solution that they appear to be missing. This desire to have the other feel better or comforted creates a major barrier to the possibility of being invited into someone's 'pit'. Chaplains are 'good' people, and they have a love for the Lord and His children. They enter this undervalued and underpaid profession with a desire to serve God and their neighbour. They want to help! They seek to make a difference in the life of the person they encounter, and this same strong desire can form the barrier to a fruitful and beneficial meeting.

I recently had a volunteer say to me:

Just so as I understand you: We follow the elements of the pastoral conversation, and this opens the possibility of an invitation into the person's 'pit'. We enter the 'pit', we listen respectfully and non-judgementally. We respond empathically to convey understanding and as a result, at the very least, comfort is transferred. Afterwards, I 'leave' their 'pit' and repeating the process, perhaps get invited into another person's 'pit'".

I replied, "Yes, that's it".

He said, "How does it help the person if they are still left in their 'pit' after I leave? What's the point of it all? Can't we do more? Can't we help them out of their 'pit'?"

I smiled at these questions because they were my questions years earlier. I thought helping meant I had to in some way make things better. My training as a counsellor had me believe that my task in helping someone was to help that person move forward; to help them progress toward some desired goal or behaviour that was currently unavailable to them. This is part of what a counsellor will do. However, this is not the aim in chaplaincy. This was my response to this student:

David, what if a person's 'pit' is the loss of a child thirty years ago, or thirty minutes ago? How do you get them out of that 'pit'? What if they have just received a terminal diagnosis from the medical staff? How do you get them out of that 'pit'? What if they have lost a leg to diabetes, and their whole independent life has suddenly come to a crushing sudden end? How do you get them out of that 'pit? The reality is you can't. You don't have that type of power. So, it's essential to be crystal clear in where our power does lie, and what is it we can do when confronted with these personal crises?

Instead, because you want to help, you start to make suggestions, or offer advice, or empty platitudes. You say something like, "You'll be fine. I know somebody who lost their leg to diabetes, and now they are back to playing golf". Or "Just pray for a miracle cure, and never give up trusting in God and the power of prayer. I've seen miracles before". Or "My aunty had the same thing, and now she is fully recovered and back to normal". It is not the task of the chaplain to offer these empty, and often annoying platitudes. Everyone else in the person's life has got these comments covered. They need and deserve something else from us. This type of response shuts the person down, who often feels unheard, misunderstood, and frankly, like they must be a fool not to realise all these silver linings surrounding their situation. Worst, this type of approach produces anxiety in all involved.

Let's say I go to speak with such a person as above, and I go in with the agenda of *doing something to make them feel better*. Its natural in this situation to feel a level of anxiety as I 'look' for any way to help the person. I'm feeling like I must help, and I am on alert as to what shape that 'help' might take. All I know is I must do something, *rather than be something*. So, I'm anxiously waiting for an opportunity to be helpful, or waiting for a sign to indicate I have been helpful, useful, productive. The patient picks up on my anxiety and retreats as the anxiety spreads between us. My goal of doing something has actually shut down the possibility of creating this God-space, and it's all over before it starts.

I have become crystal clear on *how* it is that I help, and the answer is *by creating a space where someone feels heard, understood, connected with. No advice, no solutions, no shared experiences, no apologies, no silver linings on what is happening. Just the willingness to accompany the person into the darkness and to listen in a non-anxious manner.* When I can offer that to someone, who has more than likely never experienced such a 'space' with another, in some strange, miraculous, I could even say, *Godly way*, it helps. It comforts. Patients have literally appeared younger to me after vomiting out all their suffering into this sacred space, this *God-space*. I know it works, and it's enough for me, because in truth anything else is just me *trying* to help. And when *I try* to help like that, I create a space in which I am *anxious to help*. And I keep wondering *if* I am helping or have helped. And then they hear from me all the platitudes and shallow optimisms they are hearing from everyone else who just wants themselves and the other to feel better. We chaplains must do it differently, and when we do, it's noticed and appreciated by the other person.

How can I have a non-anxious presence if I'm anxious to help someone by doing something? Yet, this calm, peaceful and attentive presence is considered of the utmost importance by the masters in the field, such as Kelly and Nouwen. It reminded me of a story involving Thomas Jefferson. In *"Thomas Jefferson: the Art of Power"*. Meacham (2012) records the first meeting between Thomas Jefferson and Mrs. Margaret Smith in the parlour of her and her husband's home. The manner in which Mrs. Smith recounts the meeting appears to have implications for the environment and substance of a chaplain's use of *presence* in interactions. In this encounter, she did not know who he was and was being hostess to this visitor while her husband was concluding some other business.

Such was his charm that though she did not know quite why, here she was, saying things she had not meant to say. "There was something in his manner, his countenance and voice that at once unlocked my heart." The caller was in a kind of control, reversing the usual order of things in which the host, not the hosted, set the terms and conditions of the conversation. "I found myself frankly telling him what I liked or disliked in our present circumstances and abode," Mrs. Smith said. "I knew not who he was, but the interest with which he listened to my artless details…put me perfectly at my ease; in truth, so kind and conciliating were his looks and manners that I forgot he was not a friend of my own. (Meacham 2012, p. 25).

I'm sure there have been many chaplains that have tried to help by *doing something rather than being something,* but as a result they have not helped, they only *think they helped* because they did something. Let's not waste the great opportunity the Lord affords us, and let's begin by going out with a willingness to enter into another's dark pit in a non-anxious, non-judgemental, peaceful manner, knowing that in this *space,* they will be comforted. In this *God-space* I have many times heard people say, "When you were able to just listen and understand me, I felt that I was aware of resources available, that before I couldn't see". They no longer feel like, "No one gets me" or "I'm all alone and no one understands what this is like". We need the skills and the courage to jump into their 'darkness', knowing we are safe, in order for a soul to unburden itself in a manner they probably never have before. "*Even though I walk through the valley of the shadow of death, I will fear no evil, for You are with me*". (Psalm 23: 4)

I will here add a short verbatim relating to one of my volunteers and their desire to 'help' a patient they visited:

One of my volunteers returned to the office after their visits, and announced, "I just had a really good conversation about a patient's fear of heights". I replied, "Okay, tell me more about that". The conversation is as follows:

Volunteer: I walked into the patient's room. It was up on the 12th floor, and I noticed that her window blind was down. I introduced myself as one of the volunteer chaplains, and I asked her if she would like the blind raised to let in some light as it was a bit dark. I could see, of course, but thought she might like some light.

Me: Go on

Volunteer: But the lady said, "No" because she has a fear of heights, and with the blind down she can forget she is up so high in the hospital. Anyway, this led us into a chat about that fear of hers. It was interesting.

Me: Andy, why did you ask the question about the blind?

Volunteer: Ummm, as I said, it was a bit dark, and I thought she might like it open.

Me: Andy, I would like you to reflect on what was going on for you by asking that question.

Volunteer: What do you mean?

Me: Well, firstly I must say that the question you asked was a bit of a disrespectful question. You see Andy, if the patient wanted the blind open, she had several options: (1) ask a staff member to do it before you arrived; (2) perhaps she could have got up and opened it herself; or (3) ask you when you came to visit. You see, I'm certain she is not incapable of doing one of those three things, and therefore, she could have dealt with that issue if she chose, if it was in fact an issue for her. However, you entered her room *unclear of what your role was*. You may not have been conscious of your desire to *do something*, but when you saw the blind down, you wanted to help by *doing* something. Remember, that we help by being available to enter their 'pit' and convey comfort through understanding. Not by providing solutions and fixes. You can't relax if you think your job is to *do something rather than be something*.

Volunteer: Right, I see what you mean. I guess I wasn't thinking about it like that.

Me: Old habits are ingrained, but this is why we have to keep reflecting on our practice.

Volunteer: At least she got a chance to talk about her fear of heights, true?

Me: Andy, you directed the conversation into her fear of heights with your question about the blind. This lady may not have had any intention to speak with anyone about her fear of heights. Remember, we let them direct the course of what is shared. It may well have been that she would have liked to speak about another wound in her heart, but that opportunity was missed, and she was forced onto a path she may not have wanted to go down. So, in my opinion, no it was not enough that she did in fact speak about her fear of heights. I think about what was potentially missed. Focus on *being* rather than *doing*.

It's such an easy trap to fall into, that of being helpful, in a very concrete manner by doing something for a patient, even on occasions when we are not asked to help. I remember an occasion in one of my CPE courses, where a fellow student was sharing a verbatim about visiting a family in the Children's Hospital. The chaplain was speaking with the mother of a child who had been in hospital for about two weeks. During their conversation, the mother expressed her concern that because of her child's hospitalisation, she had missed two weeks of a course she was doing through TAFE (Technical and Further Education) on 'Learning English'. The mother had not contacted the TAFE at this point but was concerned that her teacher at TAFE may not know the reason for her absence from the course. The chaplain then offered to ring the TAFE on her behalf. The mother agreed. When the chaplain rang the TAFE, he was asked to put the woman on the phone, and at that point the mother was able to explain the reason for her two-week absence. What follows is a verbatim of my feedback following the above scenario:

Me: Alex, why did you offer to ring the TAFE on her behalf?

Alex: Because she was concerned about the fact that TAFE didn't know why she hadn't attended in the last two weeks.

ME: Yes, I heard in your verbatim that this was a concern for her, but I didn't hear her ask you to ring the TAFE on her behalf?

Alex: No, I just offered because I wanted to help with her anxiety?

Me: Her anxiety or yours?

Alex: What do you mean?

Me: Well, you were anxious to do something to help, even when you weren't asked. The woman didn't even ask you to do this. It came from you.

Alex: Well, obviously her English was not great, so I thought it would be helpful to ring on her behalf.

Me: Alex, her English was good enough to enrol in the course in the first place, and when you did contact the TAFE, they wanted to speak to her anyway.

Alex: Well, she appreciated me doing that for her, because she said so.

Me: Well, people can be polite, and not always honest, but let's agree that she appreciated your help, that doesn't take away from the fact that you offered to do for her what she was capable of doing herself. In that regard, it's disrespectful. I think you need to reflect on what was behind your need to help in this situation, and then remind yourself how it is we do help.

Alex: I disagree. I think it was fine to offer in this situation.

At this point, I let the matter drop. If what I'm offering is not wanted or received, then I refrain from going on with it, as it would be of no use. It does however highlight just how strong the need is in some to *do something* to show that they care, or that they are useful. I always allow people to do for themselves whatever they can do for themselves. I realise I actually help no one if I do for them what they can do for themselves, let alone when I haven't even been asked to help, but assume a certain type of help is needed. My end in mind with this short manual is to develop *effective* chaplains, not chaplains who fill their days helping people by doing things for them.

Gary Collins (1995, p. 37-38) relates a story involving Henri Nouwen when he was undertaking some missionary work in Bolivia. Nouwen had been asked if he would go to a cemetery and pray with a mother whose sixteen-year-old son, Walter, had died falling off the back of a truck. This story highlights the powerlessness to which a chaplain must become accustomed too. If we do not learn to sit in the space of powerlessness in the face of so many tragedies and sufferings that we encounter, then we will be tempted to do something rather than be something. Collins writes,

When Nouwen stood with the grieving mother, next to the grave of her son, he felt overwhelmed by his inability to do anything. "I couldn't keep my eyes from the woman's face, a gentle and deep face that had known much suffering" he later wrote. "When I stood in front of the grave, I had a feeling of powerlessness and a strong desire to call Walter back to life. 'Why can't I give Walter back to his mother?' I asked myself. But then I realised that my ministry lay more in *powerlessness than in power;* I could only give her my tears".

I want to provide one further example where a chaplain may be tempted to 'jump' in and do something in order to feel like they have accomplished something. I went to visit a lady in our Older Person's Mental Health ward, let's call her Amy, who had requested a visit from a chaplain. Amy begins immediately to tell me her fears and concerns. This is often the way in Mental Health wards. Patients in these wards rarely muck around inviting you into their 'pit', it seems this is where they tend to spend the majority of their difficult lives. Amy tells me that she needs to contact her partner, because when staff got in contact with him, he told the staff member, "Tell Amy I don't want her back here. Also, I'm giving away her stuff to anyone who wants it, because I've had enough and I don't want to see her again. She won't have any stuff here, no furniture, her dog, nothing! So, there is no need for her to come back here." Amy was very angry and upset about her belongings that were being given away. She was upset about what may be happening with her little dog, and she was very scared about being homeless.

At this point, it would be very tempting for a chaplain, wanting to *do something*, to say, "Amy, I will contact the Social Worker, and they will come and see you and let you know about your housing options in this area". However, at this point, I didn't offer her the services of the social worker. I continued to just *be there and listen and empathise* with her situation. In fact, one could be forgiven for thinking this current situation was Amy's ultimate concern. It wasn't.

Amy then said to me after a short period of silence, "On the night of my daughter's 16th birthday, many years ago now, I 'shot up' heroin, passed out, and I missed her party. I had hired a little room down the street from us, and I had bought her a beautiful dress, but I missed the party. At her party, my daughter was raped by two men, and I wasn't there to protect her. The day before her seventeenth birthday she committed suicide. It was my fault. I shoulda (sic) been there".

If I had jumped in straight away to offer Amy the services of our social worker, it was very likely that Amy would not have had the opportunity to share this tragic event in her life. I would have been off to find the social worker in order to *feel like I helped*. I stayed in the 'pit' with Amy, and she invited me down to a deeper level. After Amy shared this painful wound in her heart with me, she sat there and cried on and off for 10 minutes. Amy took hold of my hand, and we just sat there in the silence as she wept over her terrible regret. After this she thanked me, and said, "I don't know where that came from. I'm sorry to dump that on you. Thank you".

Now that the *pastoral conversation had ended*, I asked Amy if she would like me to refer her to the social worker, to discuss her housing needs. There is a time and place for the chaplain to be an advocate for a patient, or to be able to make a referral to another member of the health team, but within the pastoral conversation, no.

Interestingly, one of my volunteers returned from ward visits a few days later and admitted that when a patient had spoken to them about the prospect of homelessness upon their discharge from hospital, they immediately interrupted the patient with an offer to make a referral to one of the social workers in the hospital. When I relayed my experience with Amy, they could see that in their case they were quick to offer a solution to the fear and uncertainty of the patient they were engaged with.

The desire to do something to demonstrate care and concern runs strong in chaplains, and in all fields which exist to serve their fellow man. As I have said, there is a time and place for doing something, but not when we are in the 'pit' or approaching the 'pit'.

Chaplains can serve as advocates for families and liaisons between them and the hospital staff. This function is relevant particularly in situations when family members cannot be at the bedside or the staff is unavailable, such as in the emergency department or operating room. In these situations, a chaplain can articulate family concerns to the hospital staff, as well as assist family members to process information from care providers. The chaplain is available to spend unstructured time with family members, and issues, questions, or concerns may surface that would otherwise remain unspoken. The chaplain then is able to assist the family in communicating important information to the appropriate member of the health care team, thereby preventing stress and miscommun-ication.

On occasion, I have been asked by family members to accompany them when there was a meeting between the clinical staff and the family, where decisions about care needed to be made. I am often asked to be present, and although rarely needing to say anything, my presence offered peace of mind to these families, who believed I was some sort of 'backup' in case they didn't understand something, or if they felt pressured to take some medical action that they didn't agree with.

(iv) Accepts tension areas

Unlike a typical social conversation, a pastoral conversation allows the patient to raise any issue or topic they like. In social conversations the unstated rule would normally involve keeping the conversation 'light' and more everyday issues rather than the raising of deep hurts or losses. A pastoral conversation by its nature involves the 'darker' side of a person's journey. Grundmann (2003), states:

Since anyone in despair and agony mirrors human decrepitude, such bedside ministry constantly confronts the chaplains and their own fragility. They thus experience a bit of their own dying every time when going to the bedside of people in agony.

I have found this to be true for myself, walking through the hospital. I have imagined that all these 'bombs' are going off in people's lives, and wondering, "When will it be my turn". Live long enough and I will share in their lot: that of aging, decay, loss of function, and then death. On some level, chaplains are reminded daily of their unavoidable future.

As chaplains we must be willing to listen to and by extension, be reminded of our own hurts/losses/wounds etc. This will be discussed further on when we reach the section on managing our emotional triggers, and therefore a chaplain must be able and willing to sit with a patient in some very dark places and do so in a non-anxious manner. Autton (1986, p. 118) writes:

A dying person was asked what he looked for above all in the people who were ministering to him. 'For someone to look as if they are trying to understand me', he remarked. 'He did not look for success but only that someone should care enough to try'.

As chaplains, we create a space where people can talk about things that not many other people want to hear. When we say to someone, "How are you?", we typically want a response like, "Good. And you?" If someone was to stop and start giving us a litany of problems/challenges/issues in response to that question, we would be feeling as if they had misunderstood the social etiquette behind that question. Patients can talk about their feelings and losses, their wounds, their regrets, their broken dreams and hopes. Nobody in the hospital among other professionals are going to ask, 'How do you feel about this?' They'll ask, 'Does it ache? Did you eat? Did you sleep? But with chaplains they have an opportunity to talk about how they feel. When we articulate our feelings and really get heard by someone else, spiritual healing begins. As Bernard of Clairvaux urged: 'You wish to see; listen.

Active and attentive silence

When writing of the importance of silence in a pastoral conversation, Wells (2017) states:

The final thing that's important in pastoral presence with the troubled is to say, "Is that the whole story?" Of course, it never is. It's important to stay silent for a while, to indicate that it's OK to say more. That silence is the crucial moment in the whole conversation. It's a moment of lingering, a stretching out of the hands and dwelling over the sensitive place… It's an invitation to the speaker to go deeper, where the mystery lies, and the pain resides.

When I observe people in conversations, more than ever what I have noticed is most people are very uncomfortable with silence. Whether you are at a restaurant with friends, listening to a lecture or simply having a conversation with a someone, there is an underlying pressure that most people feel to fill the space of silence. You perceive a void and feel responsible for creating some sort of response because the silence makes you squirm in your mind and body. One of the challenging aspects of beginning to date someone can be the dreaded silences. I remember in my youth, before going on a first date, I would try and think of a number of different topics I could raise if silence threatened. Yet once the relationship develops, sitting in silence together can be wonderfully intimate and powerful.

An increasing number of people are seeking silence through retreats or intentional time away from their busy lives in order to foster a spirit of "Mindfulness". But one thing they are finding is that silence is difficult, and that many people would rather do just about anything else. It can be incredibly uncomfortable to be in a space absent of distraction, precisely because we aren't distracted! We can clearly hear ourselves think, and all that is swirling around in us can be overwhelming. It's no surprise the global entertainment and media industry has revenues of over $2 trillion annually. Distraction is big business. Most people have a certain apprehension when being alone and not having anyone to talk to. It seems that silence, depriving the mind of overt stimulation, brings up all the unconscious fears, conflicts and confusions one may have.

Silence within a pastoral conversation is very important. A mental health chaplain shared the following:

It's about sharing that space ... being with that person in that place of despair. Other disciplines can't do that, because there is an outcome they need to address. I had a situation where there was a woman who had tried to hang herself several times that day, and she just told me her story, and with tears in her eyes she just talked and talked, and I did absolutely nothing. I was just there with her. I was just present.

As chaplains, we must become comfortable with periods of silence. Allowing the other to formulate the words or name the feelings can take time, and we must allow them this space. I remember a new chaplain saying to me that they felt silence in a pastoral conversation was evidence of their lack of skill or experience, and as a result, they would fill any void with words after about five seconds. I knew a chaplain of many years who was afraid that his silence may be interpreted as disapproval, indifference or agreement by the patient, and so he became anxious whenever there was a silence in his interactions.

I typically prefer to match the patient in their silence. Of course, a silence can become oppressive if it lasts too long (for me, that would be more than thirty seconds, but I do trust what my intuition is telling me about the length of any given silence) and in that situation, I will usually make an open-ended statement to ascertain where the person is at that time, for example, "I'm wondering what your feeling right now". I recommend to all new chaplains to foster a degree of tolerance for these important periods of silence. Chaplains who are tempted to fill these silence periods with questions do little to build rapport with the person. During periods of silence, patients have time to reflect, think about what they are feeling, and to feel their emotions. Chaplains must allow this reflective time to flow as a vital part of the pastoral conversation, and this fosters the quick building of rapport.

Baruth and Huber (1985) referred to "clients needing the opportunity to pause and explore their thoughts and feelings, often in silence, and the counsellor's understanding of this process can enhance the client's perception of the counsellor as a rapport-inducing agent". By honouring the space, which is created by silence, patients can start to model the chaplain in staying connected with their own emotions and that in turn helps the patient to self-empathize with their own painful feelings.

The Friend who Cares

When we honestly ask ourselves which persons in our lives mean the most to us, we often find that it is those who, instead of giving much advice, solutions, or cures, have chosen rather to share our pain and to touch our wounds with a gentle hand.

The friend who can be silent with us in a moment of despair or confusion who can stay with us in an hour of grief and bereavement, who can tolerate not-knowing, not-curing, not healing and face with us the reality of our powerlessness, that is the friend who cares.

From Henri Nouwen's book "*Out of Solitude*".

Chapter Two

Introduction to the Pastoral Care Model

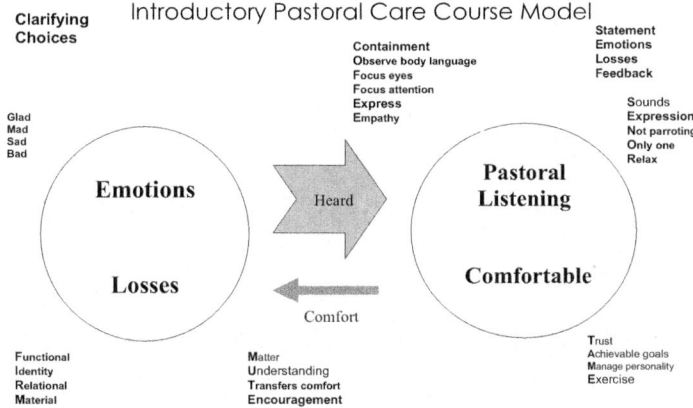

Introductory Pastoral Care Course Model

It's not for nothing TV's hospital programs are set in ERs or ORs, never the chaplain's office. Television - all media, really - prefer drama to depth, find it easier to deal with the wrenching moments of birth and death than the subtler search for the meaning of lives. I will now explain a model which highlights the important features of the pastoral care approach used in our hospital.

Clarify Choices

Clarifying choices is about an awareness of the state I'm in before I decide to head out into the hospital to visit. I need to be clear that I am in the right frame of mind to approach someone. For me, spending five to ten minutes in our hospital chapel before visiting the wards, and ensuring I'm in the right frame of mind, helps me prepare for the upcoming encounters. It's always a mistake to visit the ward in the wrong frame of mind, thinking "that it's my job, so I had better go". I ask our chaplains to have enough respect for our patients, that if we go visiting, we are ready for what may arise during those visits. This aspect also includes, for example, if your first (or whatever number visit it is) visit triggers you, and you feel a bit 'rattled', then choosing *not* to visit another patient because it's your job, is the right decision. For example, if I am a pastor of a Church, and during an important celebration for my child, a parishioner calls me, or even knocks on my front door, needing my help, it still falls to me to choose my response. That response could be, "I will come, but not now". Whatever choice we make, it's ours to make, but it's important to remember that if I choose to attend to the parishioners needs immediately, I must be ready mentally if I am to speak with that person, and if I am not ready to listen to him, then it would have been better to stay at home. Otherwise, you have only upset your family and the person in need, who will sense you are "not really there".

As well, it's important to be aware if the other person wants to be involved in a pastoral conversation at this moment? During the encounter, I would be thinking at times, "Does the other person want to end this pastoral conversation"? Do I want to end this pastoral conversation? These are all important aspects of clarifying choices.

Clarifying Choices Exercise - Pastoral Care Coordinator

Imagine you're the Pastoral Care Coordinator at your church. Have a go at thinking through these two different situations.

1. You're just being informed by a congregational member that Rose, another member of your congregation has just received tragic news - her sister has been killed in a car accident.

List the choices you might make and explain them.

_____

_____

_____

_____

_____

If you decide to make contact with Rose at some time how would you phrase your initial contact.

_____

_____

_____

_____

_____

2. Two of your grandchildren are celebrating their birthdays at your house, with your other grandchildren & children there as well. A congregational member arrives on your doorstep saying that they have been feeling very distressed for the past couple of days and would like to talk to someone.

List the choices you might make and explain them.

_____

_____

_____

_____

_____

Write down how you would phrase your choices to those concerned.

_____

_____

_____

_____

_____

Four Emotions: Glad/Mad/Sad/Bad

In Chapter 9, we will look at four main emotions I teach new volunteers when they start their work in the hospital. One could easily write up hundreds of different words to describe the emotions that humans can experience, however, to keep it as simple as possible, I use these four, which can obviously be built upon.

Glad= happy, adventurous, alive, cheerful, joyful, delighted, gleeful, etc.

Mad= angry, furious, enraged, irate, irritated, upset, hostile, impatient, etc.

Sad= depressed, miserable, anguished, detached, beat, dejected, hurt, etc.

Bad= gloomy, embittered, forlorn, heavy, guilty, ashamed, despairing, etc.

Initially, when a new chaplain is trying to consciously listen and empathise, being able to describe emotional overtones without too much angst of 'getting it right', is helpful. Over time, as we are hearing similar tales of woe, we have our favourite responses which convey that we understand or are striving too. No doubt we sometimes miss the intensity, but here is where the person 'supervises' us, and helps clarify what their depth of feeling is. For example, I may respond to someone's story, "It's so awful what has happened", and they may respond, "Awful is spilling your coffee on your outfit at the start of a day. This is absolutely devastating!". The person always guides us to a better understanding of where they are at if our intensity meter is off.

Four Losses: Functional/Identity/Relational/Material

Initially, when I began learning the effective art of chaplaincy, I was taught to be attentive to losses and feelings expressed by a person. As we saw previously, there are many different emotions we can encounter as chaplains, but at first it was far simpler to think of the four we spoke of above, and then as time goes by, to become more elegant and proficient in naming emotions. The same applies to the types of losses we encounter. So, again with ease in mind, I was trained, and in turn train new chaplains to focus on four main types of loss:

Functional: It is strongly but not exclusively associated with the ageing process. Most people react with horror to the idea of a child's blindness or crippling; yet the same phenomenon in an elderly person provokes a lesser reaction, reflecting our underlying belief that functional loss naturally goes with the ageing process. But loss is horrifying to young and old. Going blind at seventy-five is no less painful than going blind at fifteen even if it does happen more often.

Functional loss often carries with it a loss of autonomy. To lose sight or hearing or coordination is often to lose mobility. That in turn means a loss of autonomy. Gone is the sense that "I can manage." In many cases, people will admit the fact of the functional loss but will deny that some of their autonomy is lost. Aging people whose sight is failing may admit that they have cataracts but insist that they are still perfectly capable of driving a car.

When people lose a material object, they replace them. Coping with functional loss requires a comparable "way around" a restriction or handicap. It is not uncommon to discover that persons with handicaps have invented prosthetic devices to enable themselves to live normally. That is not always possible; and when it is not, the loss is often experienced as overwhelming. Amputation of a limb or breast, the discovery that one must wear a hearing aid, undergoing a colostomy- all these experiences are functional losses.

<u>Identity:</u> This loss is related to how the person sees themselves. This is such a personal and complicated aspect of who we are and is tied up with so many 'beliefs' that we have. For example, a man may believe he always needs to be the strong, capable, and solution-focused hero in order to be a "Good Husband". The same man suffers a stroke and is now no longer able to be the 'Rock' of the family and therefore his identity has been transformed. And usually in these types of occurrences, quickly. Remember the young man I mentioned with the thigh injury following his soccer Grand Final. The bulk of the loss he was experiencing was related to how he saw himself, and how others saw him.

The significance of role loss to the individual is directly related to the extent to which one's sense of identity is linked to the lost role. Retirement is perhaps the most familiar occasion of role loss, and for some people is accompanied by traumatic grief. But role loss can accompany experiences otherwise regarded as gains. Being promoted to a new level of responsibility at work also means a loss of freedom and may mean losing relationships with previous friends.

<u>Relational:</u> This loss is typically related to the loss/interruption /damage/of a relationship. People may speak of relationships they lost decades ago, of simply how an extended stay in hospital has put a strain on relationships at home, and even work. So many times, a person has described the loss of the relationships that have been developed through the workplace, and how an unwanted or sudden illness results in a massive whole in their relational life.

It is an unavoidable component of human life. Sooner or later we all experience such a loss. It may be partial, as in moving five hundred miles away, or total, as with widowhood. One man, recently divorced, admits that what he misses most is the fights he had with his former wife. Pastoral work with those who have gone through a divorce is essentially grief counseling, though it may have other focal points as well.

Relationship loss may be temporary or permanent, but it always comes. Even when the relationship loss is a part of the process of growing up, it can nevertheless be a painful experience of grief. Death ends opportunities to engage in a wide variety of forms of relating oneself to others. It is generally the most intense form of relationship loss. Death may require that a person sort through memories, address remarks to the departed person, acknowledge the pain, anger, guilt, and other feelings that may be present: in short, carry on an internal dialogue with oneself, the dead person, and others.

Material: This loss is related to the material, often financial loss of a stay in hospital, especially an extended stay. Again, recall our young soccer player who faced up to 12 months rehabilitation before even the prospect of returning to work arose. As a young father and homeowner, he was very scared about the financial situation he and his family found themselves in.

Some adults resist recognizing the importance of material loss, as if to take it seriously might mean that one was either too materialistic or too sentimental. Children will much more easily confess how strong their attachment to a particular object is, and how painful its loss.

Most human beings have some kind of powerful attachment to a material object, whether it be a family farmhouse or a favourite jacket. If the farmhouse is one day bulldozed to the ground or the jacket given to the Salvation Army, either is a painful loss. If the object is important because of its origin – a gift, say, from someone deeply loved – it has extrinsic value. Other objects may have an intrinsic value; we have an investment in them for some quality of their own. Objects with extrinsic value attached to another human being whom we love, cause the deepest pain when lost.

Many persons who have undergone material loss report an almost irresistible urge to replace the lost object. In some cases where a comparable replacement is impossible because of the expense, a copy or some other symbolic replacement is substituted. Those who replace lost material objects often conclude that the replacement is never quite the same as the original, even when by objective standards it is better in quality or costs more.

Material loss is frequently, though not universally, the first loss of which the child is consciously aware. Early material losses take familiar forms; the scoop of ice cream that falls from the cone, the toy broken too badly, to be mended, the soft ball confiscated by an angry neighbor. From an adult's point of view, such losses are easily replaced. But if a caring adult fails to take the child's sense of loss seriously, and emphasizes the ease of replacement, the child may construct a fantasy world in which all lost objects can be replaced. This is untrue; and when the child discovers that fact, the sense of loss is compounded.

The fact that some material losses are replaceable may mask the grief reaction accompanying any loss. The grief may show through only in the sense that the replacement is never quite so good as the original. The loss of a pet is an occasion of grief for adults as well as for children. The intensity of the grief is not surprising. The relationships between people and their pets are charged with quasi-human characteristics, so that we feel that our pets are almost human. And yet grief over the death of a pet has several striking characteristics of material loss. Most people immediately replace a lost pet even while saying the original pet is irreplaceable. We talk about pets as though losing them is a relationship loss, but we treat pets, in the long run, as material objects.

When I am training new chaplains, I have them pay attention to the four feelings and four losses that a person may share. I tell them that if they hear a loss, ask themselves "What's the feeling behind that loss?" If they hear a feeling, ask themselves, "What's the loss behind that feeling?", and then feedback to the person. In this manner, one can put an end to the problem of parroting back at someone. For example, someone says, "I am so sick and tired of the continual train of people who keep walking into my room". If I attend directly to the feeling, I will border on being a parrot, for example, "It sounds like you've had enough of all the interruptions". However, if I think about the feelings: frustration, resentment, anger, impatience, and I ask myself what's the loss behind these emotions is, I could respond, "It sounds like you are really missing the privacy and control you had when you're at home, and here, you seem to have none of that". Obviously, there are many different responses, but I identify the feelings, and try and identify the loss and feedback that. I would typically get a response from the person along the lines of, "Exactly, I'm just sick of this place and want to go home".

Matter/Understanding/Transfers Comfort/Encouragement

Matter:

They and their story matters to you and God. This is just such a powerful thing to remember. As chaplains we 'represent' God in our workplace, and I have had chaplains dislike that description of us as His representative. I would go further and say we are "God with skin on in the hospital", which I'm sure could make some cringe, but I never minded the reminder that when we introduce ourselves as 'Chaplains' people see us in some way connected with God/religion /Faith etc.

Many people have had poor experiences with their Church or with ministers, therefore it's a powerful opportunity for us as chaplains to arrive to speak with a patient and have that experience be a positive one. This is not the time to push our agenda, or try and "save' a person, it's the time to create the God-space and use the skills we have learnt to enable the person to feel understood and connected with. Leaving such an impression will only encourage the person to seek out a chaplain the next time they feel one is needed. We as chaplains have to trust that God loves this person more than us, and so 'saving' them is on God, not us!

Understanding:

When we respond using empathic language, we convey to that person we understand or are striving to understand their situation. This has a powerful effect on people. Within this unique 'space' people who feel connected and understood are able to recognise their own strengths, hopes, solutions etc. It truly is amazing how this happens. People at the start of a conversation may indeed be oblivious to options/ their strengths/ possible options they have etc, and yet through our willingness to enter the darkness through empathic responding, it's like the 'fog' lifts and these qualities and options reveal themselves to the person. I have heard more than once, "After speaking with you, I can see now that I do have other options. Thank you so much for coming to see me". A person in pain is helped the moment he senses that he/she is being understood.

<u>Transfers Comfort:</u>

Doesn't it feel wonderful to be heard and understood. When I first started as a chaplain, one of my personal challenges was the cold-call introduction to a patient on the ward. It was quite a vulnerable feeling to approach a person who had not requested to see me, make an offer to visit and talk, and then have the next few moments filled with uncertainty: will it be "yes, sit down", or "No, leave me alone". Maybe to someone who isn't a chaplain in a hospital, this doesn't appear too daunting, but I don't know any chaplains who haven't struggled with the 'Cold-Call'. For me, what helped in this area was some simple reframing: I would say to myself as I headed to the ward, "I am about to offer someone a truly wonderful gift: the gift to be really heard, valued, respected, understood, and as far as possible within myself, not judged. Who wouldn't love that?" *IF* that is not needed at that time, or my offer is not seen in that light, then that's fine, and I walk on. However, that little reframe that I repeated each time I approached the next bed, helped me deal with that little voice in my head that said, "What are you doing. You don't like it if a Jehovah Witness turns up on your doorstep on a Saturday morning uninvited and unannounced, so why do it to this person. Can't you God-bothers just wait to be called before you go out and try and save the world?" You can easily appreciate that approaching a person with this negative 'voice' in my head can easily translate into my body language in such a manner that I can receive a lot of "No, thanks" from people when making my offer. Again, once I have clarified my choice to attend the ward, the responsibility is on me to 'get my head in the right space', especially given that what occurs between my ears is largely up to me. Also, if we chaplains waited to be paged or called to visit a patient, we would sit in our office a lot. Most people are unaware that they need us to sit and listen to their story, and it often only becomes a possibility once a social conversation has started following a cold-call, and something tells the person this chaplain, this *intimate stranger* can be trusted to '*hold*' something they have carried for so long, and never felt they could share with another person.

As mentioned, through the use of empathic responses I have witnessed and heard how what we do comforts at the low end and transforms at the upper end. Even in a social conversation people can be comforted to just know that they had a visitor. So many patients have no visitors, especially during Covid-19, when virtually no patients were allowed visitors.

Encouragement:

The impact of pastoral listening and being comfortable is that the person we are engaging with is encouraged to find their own solutions and resources, through the companionship that comes about in the 'pit'. That feeling of not being alone, of being understood is so powerful, that all manner of strategies/hopes/and healing can take place.

Trust/Achievable Goals/Manage Personality/Exercise

Trust:

Trust the process. Trust the practical results of those who came before you. Trust that people who are more experienced, and that have a solid position of reflective practice have seen the results of this training. Is it different to what you expected? Yes. Is it contrary to what you have always thought was good enough and sufficient? Yes. I remember it was the start of a one of my 400 hr CPE courses, and the facilitator of that group announced, "All you really have to do to be successful as a chaplain is to be yourself". I responded, "With respect, if that's all it is, if I promise to just be myself, can I get the certificate today, and skip the next 8 months being here?" You see, it's so much more than just being yourself. For example, I want an engineer to be himself whilst building a bridge, but I also require him to have the skills necessary to build the bridge safely as he's being himself. It's this short-sighted attitude to chaplaincy that I have found plagues this small field. "Just be nice, be affirming, be kind, have a bible passage or two to throw at someone, find the positive, etc". This role is too important to miss just how essential the acquisition of skills is: here no different to the engineer. Put your own self perceived attitudes/beliefs/practices aside and try something that works. *Processus credere!*

Achievable goals:

Changing any habit takes time and adopting a new way of engaging with someone does not arrive all of a sudden. I remember learning to drive a car for the first time: so much to be conscious of. So many things to remember with the car-use the seat belt, use of mirrors, eye on the speedo, lane position, location of other vehicles, etc. Then all the road rules to recall and know when and how to implement them. Plus, all of this was in an automatic vehicle. Once I decided to learn in a manual vehicle, there was a whole lot of new things to learn about the clutch, releasing the clutch, the different gears, when to use which gear, and of course, the dreaded hill starts and stops in a manual vehicle in order not to stall. It's all so deliberately conscious, and it takes time for us to become unconsciously competent drivers (although it's obvious some never reach that level). The same is true with this approach here. It takes time to be able to hear the loss/emotions, imagine what that must be like if it was happening to you, and feedback an elegant empathic response in about three seconds! So, don't set your task to master this approach in a week or two. Cathy worked me very hard in the adoption of skills when I started, and I noticed it began to become more natural after about 6 months of 30 hours/week. Don't be put off by that though, as you may get it faster than me. Just have a reasonable expectation of your ability to engage effortlessly in a pastoral conversation in a state of being completely relaxed and confident.

Manage Personality:

Managing your own frustrations/fears or other concerns as you acquire these essential skills in becoming an effective chaplain can be challenging. It was for me. I have high expectations, and so I had to deal with the frustrations of feeling that I was not 'getting' this as fast as I would have liked. Also, I wanted the approval of my mentor, and so as we practiced role-plays, or critiqued my verbatims, I was aware that my responses were at a very basic level. I was containing all the elements of the social conversation, but when I listened to the responses of my mentor, I realised how far I had to go. I wanted to be able to do what I was doing at a higher, more natural level, like my mentor. However, it was my task to realise that my mentor had been practicing this art for more than a decade, and that it takes time to build a set of new skills, and also to begin to do all the inner work that was required to be really present for another as they shared their sorrows and concerns. So, don't be in too much of a rush, and manage your frustrations and mistakes with a gentle hand.

As chaplains who typically work in teams, we must also learn to manage how we feel when we hear what other chaplains are saying and doing out on the wards. Some chaplains return very excited about how they were able to 'help' someone by offering a fix or putting a silver-lining around a problem, and I have to manage how I respond to that. Usually I don't respond at all, because my end in mind would be to bring about a shift in their practice of chaplaincy, and if that is unlikely or futile, then I keep my mouth shut. I do what I can do, and they do what they believe is the right way to do things. A chaplain returned to the office and said to another chaplain, "I spoke with this lady about so many different problems she was having: problems with her health, problems with her husband, problems with her grown children. I just told her to hand it all over to God, and He would help". In my mind I was thinking, "If this woman was a woman of faith, then she would know she could hand it over to God, and if she wasn't a woman of faith, then your comment meant nothing to her". The only real control I have over anyone is myself, so I practice the skills I have learnt, and others will offer what they have. It's up to me to manage my response to chaplains who in my mind, are just out offering solutions and bible passages to patients in crisis.

Exercise:

Practice the skills. Opportunities arise everywhere for pastoral conversations. I had lots of exercise in the practice of these skills outside my workplace. I found as a result that many, if not all of my relationships improved. For example, if my wife came home and said to me, "I just hate the way my boss treats me at work. He must think I'm a child, because he just micromanages me, and it makes it harder to get my work done". In the past, thinking it was job to always be the problem solver, I would respond, "Honey, just walk in there tomorrow and tell him you've had enough of being micromanaged, and that you don't need that level of attention to do your job". My wife would just shake her head as she walked off, and I would think, "You've done it again champion. Another crisis averted". After learning this model, and realising people are capable of coming up with their own solutions, I recalled what my dad said to me the day I got married: My dad asked me if I thought my wife-to-be was not only beautiful, but smart as well? I said, "Of course". He said, then when she comes to you with a problem, just say, "Oh, that's awful. Tell me more about it". Don't just give her your solution, like she is incapable of finding the answers herself". It was apparent that I had forgotten that piece of wisdom, and I had slipped easily into my 'Mr Fixer' role within our marriage. In general, I have stopped responding like this, but I am aware there are occasions when exhaustion overrides my developing abilities, and when I hear a problem, I can simply shoot a solution at her. But at least I am aware, and then I say to my wife that I am too tired for conversing right now, but perhaps later on or tomorrow I can hear what's going on for you. My wife respects the honesty, and I always remember to follow up on our arranged talk.

Sounds/Expressions/Not Parroting/Only One/Relax

Sounds/Seems:

When responding in a PC, I train our volunteers to start their response with either, "It sounds like…" or "It seems…" For example, a patient states, "I can't stand being unable to get up and go to the toilet myself. They keep the bed rails up, and I have to buzz and wait for staff to come and escort me to the bathroom. Sometimes they take forever to come and you know….I don't want any accidents". You could respond, "It sounds like you're missing the little things we all take so much for granted". This approach, which is very suitable when beginning, is a gentle way of 'testing the water'. Again, stating, "It sounds like you're angry", is preferable to "You're angry". It allows the other an opportunity for clarity of confirmation, but at the same time, respectful and gentle.

Expressions:

I emphasise to new chaplains just how important the expression on our face is when we offer a response. The expression must match our response. In fact, there are many times when an expression combined with a short sound like, 'Hmmm' is more than enough to convey that you get them and that you are understanding. There are times when, especially for a new chaplain/volunteer, they are lost for words, and they are not sure how to respond. These times are perfect to say nothing, have the right expression combined with a short sound, and that will in many ways be better than just trying to 'throw a line out there' in order to say something.

Not Parroting:

We already touched on this in the section regarding losses and emotions.

Only One:

It often happens that we are talking with someone who mentions a number of losses or emotions or both, and sometimes we can be tempted to respond to each individual part of what they have just said. This is unnecessary, as all we have to do is respond to one part of what they have said in order to convey that we have heard and are seeking to understand the situation. For example:

Imagine you are having morning tea after church and you ask a friend, "How are things going?"

They respond, "Well actually not very well. My house was robbed on Tuesday. Not only did they take what you would expect, camera, some cash that was lying around but for some reason they took a lot of my family photos. I tell you if I had been given half the chance, I would have strangled the ratbags. Though at the moment I'm just feeling pretty low because (pause) to be honest I'm even a bit nervous about staying in the house by myself at the moment."

As you can see there are a few different losses and emotions going one here. One possible response could be:

"It does sound scary. Your home is meant to be a safe place but at the moment it doesn't seem safe at all!"

Relax:

Fortunately, the vast majority of people we meet have no idea how poorly others communicate. So, why we are learning to become more consciously competent at the beginning, remember, they don't know any better themselves. So, relax, and focus on the other, and over time like everything, you will improve, your responses will become more elegant, and sound more natural. Remember, a large part of putting these skills into practice means you are not afraid to enter the 'darkness' of the other. Learning to be comfortable with the uncomfortable is an important aspect of learning these skills. No one likes to be afraid, and so we will avoid scary situations unless we become comfortable with the things in our own past that scare us or makes us feel less than. Autton (1986, p. 117) states when talking about those who help others in a crisis:

They have come to terms with their own spiritual distress when confronted with another's pain; their own emotional strengths and weaknesses have to be explored and understood if they are to exercise an enabling and supportive ministry. They will be *blind* to other's needs if their own anxiety and insecurity are too intense when faced with ontological questions. *If they are in discomfort in the situation, carers will have a tendency to distance themselves from the sufferer.*

Statements/Emotions/Losses/Feedback

This is the heart of the pastoral conversation: that is, as I listen and hear the 'groan' of the patient, I imagine what it would be like to experience this situation, and I'm listening to whether the person is sharing their crisis by using either emotions or losses to describe what it's like for them, and then I feedback to them an empathic statement in order to convey understanding. Once more, if the person expresses a feeling, I ask myself, "What is the loss behind this feeling?" If they express a loss, I ask myself, "What is the feeling behind this loss?". Sometimes, a person will give a lot of information, containing a variety of feelings and losses. In this case, just pick one that either stands out to you, or seems like the dominant feeling or loss. In another instance, I had a patient express so many losses in this way:

I'm in a terrible way now. I came into the hospital and the doctor took me off all my medications and put me on something new. That may be good for my body, but I'm sad, and my depression has become a lot worse. It's the worst it's been. I'm angry I'm here still and I haven't felt this depressed since I lost my husband. I am all alone. I'm so lonely. I lost him about four years ago, and he was the love of my life. We were married for 55 years. It was terrible to lose someone you have been with since you were 25 years old. No one is visiting me, none of my friends or family. I have a son who has a brain injury, and needs looking after, whom I'm so worried about, and another son who was born with a brain abnormality, so they can't visit, and I suffer terribly with pain in my body, especially my legs, and now I am so depressed. My husband would have been here to support me, but he died, and my only sister died two years ago. What else can I tell you?

I responded:

I can't think of anything else you could tell me that would help me understand any better than you already have, just how much you have suffered these last few years.

A friend of mine who runs Accidental Counselling Training for school- teachers, has shared the above pattern of communicating with his student-teachers, for the simple reason that this method builds rapport quickly. For teachers this is so important, because when we build rapport with another person, then we have established a mutual relationship where consideration, respect and empathy can flourish. Remember: rules without relationship leads to rebellion. You can see then how important it is for a teacher who has to enforce certain rules, to prefer their students comply because of the relationship they have, rather than have a rebellious classroom where no learning can occur.

In the hospital, the situation is just as important, but for another reason: we don't often have a lot of time with our patients. Most hospital chaplain will have one, maybe two visits to create the *God-space*, where wounds and 'emotional baggage' can be faced and shared. As a result, a chaplain must build rapport quickly, otherwise opportunities will be lost, for if a chaplain should return to visit a patient, they often find that the person has been discharged. Of course, there are wards where patients may remain longer in the system, such as Mental Health, but building rapport quickly is beneficial whether you are a hospital chaplain, or a schoolteacher, or a salesman. It has been said that a person's favourite topic is themselves, and it was Dale Carnegie, in his classic book, *How to Win Friends and Influence People*, who said, when people look at a photo that they are in, they always look at themselves first. Being person-focussed and combining the Statement/Emotion/Loss/Feedback method, rapport is built quickly, and that creates a wonderful opportunity for something miraculous to occur between the chaplain and the Other.

Statements:

Just make statements using "It sounds like" or "It seems like". This approach is a gentle way to offer feedback back to the other. I have found that asking a lot of questions during a visit is an indicator of being uncomfortable. I have had new chaplains say to me, "It's hard to practice these skills when I only visit the hospital for two hours a week". My response is to ask them to see every conversation they have as an opportunity to practice our empathic responses. I challenge them to have a conversation with someone and to see just how much they can learn about the person by *NOT* asking questions. I tell them they will be surprised. Practice making statements and not asking questions, and this will go along way to creating rapport and enabling the God-space to become a reality.

Emotions:

Be attentive to emotions expressed, and emotions hidden behind body language. Paul Ekman made his life's work the effort to be able to spot concealed emotions. His book *Telling Lies* is a classic in the field. It turns out to be very difficult to detect lies reliably, but Paul did improve the odds a little with training that he developed for the CIA and the FBI. And along the way, he discovered something fascinating: when we're concealing a strong emotion, we almost always let it out in "micro-expressions," sudden leakages of the emotion that are expressed in our faces, unbeknownst to ourselves – and mostly to the people around us, for very brief flashes of time – as little as a 24th of a second. For example, Flared nostrils may show aggression or disapproval. Or they can indicate that the person is making a judgment about something.

Losses:

Listen for the expressed losses. Glenn Boyd (2003) when writing of the importance listening plays in what we do as pastoral care workers states:

The most important thing pastoral counsellors do is listen carefully to their clients. That formula may sound simplistic, but everything else we do as professional helpers depends on the value placed on listening. Unless we learn to value listening, we will not learn to value those with whom we work or ourselves, for that matter. Listening comprises a number of related attitudes and behaviours and, in fact, probably requires some degree of natural giftedness for empathy that can be learnt but cannot be taught.

Feedback:

Remember, hear a loss, feedback the emotion. Hear an emotion, feedback the loss. The Other is always our supervisor within the context of the encounter, so if we miss intensity, or name an emotion which is not accurate, they will correct us. The whole time however they will be feeling like we are 'with them' and striving to understand what it's like for them to be going through this particular crisis.

When the pastoral conversation is over, usually because the person has indicated that it is over by saying something like, "Thank you so much for listening. I'm sorry that I dumped all that on you", I will typically say something like, "Thank you so much for sharing your story with me". I may offer to say a prayer if they have mentioned God, but otherwise I will usually not offer a prayer at the bedside. So, as a rule, the patient ends the time in the 'pit', although there are times when staff or a fire alarm will bring the conversation to an end. If I'm with a patient who is going over and over the same story, I will also wait for a break in the conversation, and say something like, the above statement, as our time is precious, and if a patient is 'stuck in a loop' with no additional information being shared, then I need to bring this conversation to an end in order to be available to other patients. This repeating of the same story over and over is more akin to a moan then a groan, and as no new information is given, then we need to take action to end this type of conversation.

Containment/Observe Body language/Focus Attention/Focus eyes/Express Empathy

Containment:

I spoke about this previously: contain all the aspects of a social conversation when you have entered into a pastoral conversation. There are a lot of aspects of our normal, social, way of communicating that we have to contain. This containment will take time to perfect but is the foundation of the pastoral conversation.

Observe Body Language:

Research in this area assures us that typically over 90% communication comes from body language. This is comforting, because it implies if we get the body language right, we are already 90% conveying we are respectfully listening, and striving to understand. Most of the time, our body language is unconscious. We move naturally in certain ways without even noticing. This means we're sending signals all the time, even if we're unaware of them. By being able to understand our own and other people's body language signals, we can improve our communication on a wide scale. Be mindful of your body language when you're with someone, and what messages you may or may not be sending. I had a staff member that came to see me in my office, and they dropped in regularly just to say, "Hi" and gossip about hospital matters. After they left on this occasion, one of my colleagues commented, "Wow! If looks could kill". I responded, "What are you talking about?" He replied, "You just looked really irritated as you were sitting listening to her". I, of course, had no idea that that was the 'look' and vibe I was putting out. In our training, to emphasise the importance of body language, we use a number of exercise which exaggerates inappropriate body language. For example:

Focus Attention: Body Language Exercise
Maintain focus on the other. Obviously, this is an aspect of
Role Play 1 'Itchy Everything'
Your mission is to keep moving around but still. Try and keep reasonable eye contact.
Suggestions:

Scratch your head – change arms & do the other side of your head.
Scratch your neck, sides, back, elbows, legs but try to keep looking at the other person.
If the other person says something like "Are you all right?" Respond with something like "Sure, fine. Please go on, I'm listening" and keep on moving!
Move in your seat and then move the whole seat a few times a little bit.
Stretch.
Your clothes are just not right - keep adjusting them. But keep looking at the person speaking - Nodding your head.
Exercises like this are a good way to demonstrate that a lack of awareness of your body language will have a negative impact on your encounter with anyone.

Maintain focus on the other. Obviously, this is an aspect of 'Observe Body Language'. I have found that often in a hospital ward there is a lot going on, a lot of noises, staff coming and going, visitors coming and going, a lot of distractions. Endeavour in this busy environment to stay focussed on the patient. If you keep looking up at the many different people and sounds that are occurring, the person will soon get the hint that you are not really focussed on them. This means that the likelihood of the person sharing something of ultimate concern is dramatically reduced. Nobody enjoys feeling like the person they are speaking with is easily distracted or worse, appearing to listen, but not really. I myself have been guilty of this, and even worse, caught looking at my watch. We are all a work in progress, but these are aspects of our visiting that must be controlled, as they send a powerful message of disinterest.

Express Empathy:

I often joke that I am in the Empathy Business, except it's no joke. A chaplain working in a hospital/Prison/Nursing Home etc, has quite a few different duties, from conducting religious services, providing Sacraments where possible, offering prayers for the dying, but by far and away our main task is to visit people and engage with them. Empathy is our 'bread and butter'. Empathy builds rapport rapidly and opens the way for much deeper connection. When I'm listening to someone speak of their suffering, I imagine to myself, "What if I was going through this? How would I feel?" That question brings up possible emotions and losses, and then I feed that back to the person. As humans we have similar responses to the unfortunate things that can happen to us. Therefore, in most cases, what I imagine would be going on for me, is very close to what is happening for the Other. When I offer a person empathy, they feel heard and understood.

There are times when before empathy, I use compassion. For example, let's say I went to the ward just after lunchtime, and I meet a patient who says, "They brought me my lunch, but there are no utensils. So, although I'm starving, I can't eat the blessed thing". If I respond, "How frustrating to want to eat so badly, but you can't even though it's right under your nose. Like being tortured". Not much use, right? It would be far better first to say, "Let me see if I can go and get you some utensils so you can finally eat your lunch", then try and empathise.

Chapter Three

Impact of Pastoral Listening and Being Comfortable

It doesn't have to be the blue iris.

It can be a weed in a vacant lot

Or a few small stones: Just pay attention.

Mary Oliver.

Practicing Pastoral Listening Exercise

Richard & Terry

Richard (aged 60) & Terry (aged 40) are entering the church grounds on a Sunday morning at the same time. Terry has heard on the very effective church grapevine that Richard is about to enter hospital for a major operation. After they greet each other, Terry asks "How you feeling about the operation?"

Richard keeps walking, "OK I guess."

"Well," Terry goes on, "I just want you to know that I'm praying for you. Also, my uncle had the same sort of operation and he is doing really well and I bet that you're probably quite a bit fitter than ..."

"Terry, " Richard has stopped walking and is looking at Terry, "I appreciate your concern but I would just like to focus on my worship of God at the moment." Richard not waiting for a reply walks into church.

Terry annoyed, thinks to himself - *I was only trying to be supportive - no need to cut me off mid sentence especially when I'm trying to encourage him. I wonder if he is losing his faith. I think I had better mention this to my Bible Study group.*

Terry could have handled this encounter with Richard differently.

List some of them.

_____

_____

_____

_____

_____

Richard also could have handled this situation differently. List some of them.

_____

_____

_____

_____

_____

The impact of pastoral listening and being comfortable is powerful. Contemporary culture devalues listening, probably because it is a culture of doing, a get-it-done-yesterday mindset that frames speaking as power and listening as weakness. Few people listen well, believing that what they are doing is 'good' listening. However, most people are not in fact listening, but actively thinking about how to respond, and usually with solutions and platitudes. This is not listening, and furthermore, it produces anxiety. Glenn Boyd (2003) when defining listening states:

One dictionary defines "listen" this way: 1) to give attention with the ear; attend closely for the purpose of hearing; give ear, 2) to pay attention; heed; obey, 3) to wait attentively for a sound (Random House Unabridged). This definition emphasizes the word *"attention"* in a way that suggests something we might miss in the daily habit of listening. Listening is selective. If one does not tune out a great deal of competing noise, one would go crazy. To listen is to focus on what one chooses to hear, even if it is a highly conditioned choosing. Because choosing seems to happen automatically, it is easy to forget that one is continually filtering out an almost infinite number of possible distractions. Listening is an act of will. One can be considerably more conscious about listening by simply choosing to do so.

When we utilise the elements of pastoral listening, we communicate to the Other something incredible: we communicate that not only do they matter, including what they are going through and what they feel, but because this comes from a chaplain, the message is *they matter to God.* This can be transformative to a person who may feel that they have never really mattered to God.

How many souls do we meet who in one way of another feel that they have lived in God's blind spot. Prayers unanswered, dreams coming to naught, hopes dashed, and yet trying to make sense of this lived experience with the belief in an All loving, All-Powerful God. Now in their current crisis, a chaplain visits, often out of the blue, and representing God, listens, empathises, and understands (or at least tries), and suddenly this person feels that God sees and hears them. This itself is comforting if not transformative. The chaplain understands, therefore God understands. The chaplain listens, therefore God listens. I'm important to the chaplain, therefore I'm important to God. In this realisation there is a healing of the soul in many instances, and this, as I mentioned before, can be seen in the change that takes place in the face and energy that is emitted from such a person. From this space, this *God-space*, comes hope, solutions, forgotten resources, a freshness of what tomorrow may bring now.

From Henri Nouwen's book "Out of Solitude" comes The Friend who Cares:

When we honestly ask ourselves which persons in our lives mean the most to us, we often find that it is those who, instead of giving much advice, solutions, or cures, have chosen rather to share our pain and to touch our wounds with a gentle hand.

The friend who can be silent with us in a moment of despair or confusion who can stay with us in an hour of grief and bereavement, who can tolerate not-knowing, not-curing, not healing and face with us the reality of our powerlessness, that is the friend who cares.

Nouwen, in *The Wounded Healer*, speaks of 'hospitality' as the place where healing happens. I like the use of this phrase. It conjures up creating a space for a visitor in which my attention is on them as I serve their needs. Nouwen goes on to state:

"Hospitality is the virtue that allows us to break through the narrowness of our own fears and to open our houses to the stranger, with the intuition that salvation comes to us in the form of a tired traveller. Hospitality makes anxious disciples into powerful witnesses, makes suspicious owners into generous givers, and makes closed-minded sectarians into interested recipients of new ideas and insights. What does hospitality as a healing power require? It requires first of all that the hosts feel at home in their own house, and second, that they create a free and fearless place for the unexpected visitor. (p. 95)

One notices that Nouwen states, "First of all that the host feel at home in their own house". This leads to a comfortability that is essential to the space required where transformations take place. Of course, it has to do with being comfortable in our own darkness, with our own triggers and wounds, and then being clear about how it is we help in a pastoral encounter. I have spoken about this earlier, but I cannot emphasis how important this aspect is. Another important feature of this comfortability is trusting that God is with us in these encounters: He is there before I arrive, whilst I am there, and after I leave. Trusting in His presence and love for the Other (and myself), and knowing that He is behind all transformations, leaves me with the understanding that I do not want to get in His way, but be the channel in that moment where He can act in the life of one who desperately needs Him in their crisis.

Chapter Four

Expressing Empathy: What it is NOT

I want to start with a scenario which I give to all new students. The very first thing I do with any new group of students is give them the following scenario and ask for their responses. It always provides a valuable insight into where these students are coming from, and their responses help form the basis of the difference between how we normally respond to somebody in crisis, and how we respond utilising the elements of the PC. The scenario:

Imagine you are having morning tea after church and you ask a friend, "How are things going?"

They respond, "Well actually not very well. My house was robbed on Tuesday. Not only did they take what you would expect, camera, some cash that was lying around but for some reason they took a lot of my family photos. I tell you if I had been given half the chance I would have strangled the ratbags. Though at the moment I'm just feeling pretty low because (pause) to be honest I'm even a bit nervous about staying in the house by myself at the moment."

Write down what you would say to your friend at this time.

_____

_____

_____

_____

I have had many different responses to this scenario, some good, most average, a few really bad ones. Some examples of the average to bad responses:

1. Have you checked with insurance to see what can be replaced?
2. Have you asked relatives who may have copies of some of your photos?
3. Have you changed your locks?
4. Don't be scared. Robbers don't return to the scene of the crime to often…do they?
5. My uncle trains guard dogs and that would help you feel safe. I can give you his number.
6. Would you like to stay with me for a few nights?

One can see that with all these responses, the listener is trying to help. These responses come from a heart which wants to make things better, but the problem is they don't. In fact, most people would easily come up with these fixes on their own, but because we need to feel as though we have helped, that we have eased their anxiety/pain/suffering, we offer solutions. We want to feel better, so we have to make them feel better. It's how we have been socially taught to deal with grief.

Practicing Pastoral Listening: <u>What Empathy is Not!</u>

Asking Questions	"How did they get in?" "Was your camera insured?" "How can I help? You can stay at my place?"
Your Experiences	"When I was robbed they took some of my photos as well" "I know how you feel I've been robbed six times in the last few years"
Your Cheer Up Thoughts & Encouragements	"At least you weren't attached & hurt" "You never know you may still get them back." "Remember God's with you & he will look after you."
Your Advice	"Why don't you call your family & see if they have some copies." "It doesn't help getting over worried." "Why don't we pray & see what God does."
Your Interpretation	"You are probably so upset because

(Your Imagination)	some of the photos were of your mother and your still grieving over her death from last year" "I think God may be trying to say something to you about worldly possessions."
Your Sympathy	"I'm so sorry." "I'm so sad to hear that." "I feel so angry as well."
Your Agreement	"I think you ought to punch their heads in." "I would be scared as well."

I wonder as you read these responses can you imagine saying the same kind of things? Ask yourself, "Why would I respond like this?" "What's my end in mind with this type of response?" How have I felt when others have offered me solutions and platitudes when I have been in my 'pit'?"

I remember breaking up with my first girlfriend, and I was very upset, and my dad said, "You will be happy this girl broke up with you when you meet the next girl". At that moment in time, that comment was not helpful, and in fact, I thought to myself that my dad has no clue how much this girl means to me. I had no thought or desire for "the next girl", I wanted this girl. My dad wanted to help me get through this by offering me a silver-lining on this large dark sad cloud that had overshadowed my whole life, or that's how at least it felt. Nothing anybody was going to do was going to make this situation better, but it would have been comforting if someone, a friend or family member, could have tried to understand what this break-up meant for me. What if someone had been able to say, "Anything I say would just sound so hollow, because for you, your heart is broken, and it and life will never be the same again. Who you are has been altered forever, and right now, there is no sunshine or happiness in this life". Wow! What a difference that would have made. I would've wanted more of that empathy, like the very oxygen I was breathing. When you are with someone who is in their 'pit', put aside any idea that your fixes will help, and strive for understanding and offer them that response. This is where your own sufferings can help formulate an empathic response. Draw on your own sufferings, your own woundedness, and respond with the feelings and losses that arise from those experiences. When you respond like this, you literally stand out from the crowd, and that person will not be able to forget the gift you gave them when they were at 'rock-bottom'. Doris Zagdanski in *Stuck for Words*, states, "When good listening and empathy are combined they are dynamite-they can help to release built up grief".

Scenario Response Exercise

A group of friends are having their regular lunch together.

Sandra is asked how Jim her husband is going. Everyone is aware that Jim has recently been made redundant by the company he has been part of for many years. Sandra is feeling anxious as she is thinking that this is a side of Jim that she has never seen before.

Sandra	Well, he seems to have lost a lot of his normal motivation to do things; he is watching a lot of TV which is not really like him.
Responses:	I think you ought to take him to the doctors
	I'm sure he will feeling better soon
	When my Bill got sacked, I told him to get off his backside & don't stop looking until you find another one.
	Bit scary, this is not the Jim you know & love.
	How is the money holding up?

On the basis of the responses only, which of her friends is Sandra more likely to seek out to talk with one to one?

Chapter Five

Expressing Empathy: What it looks like

Carl Rogers stated this about the use of empathic listening:

It means entering the private perceptual world of the other and becoming thoroughly at home in it. It involves being sensitive, moment by moment, to the changing felt meanings which flow in this other person, to the fear or rage or tenderness or confusion or whatever that he or she is experiencing. It means temporarily living in the other's life, moving about in it delicately without making judgements.

Empathy is a statement feeding back what you think is the speaker's emotion and loss. Even though empathy has the listener speaking it is still part of the pastoral listening process. When we empathise, hopefully we are still being quick to listen not quick to speak. Put simply, empathy is the ability to step into another person's shoes and feel what they feel. Moshin Hamid described empathy as "finding echoes of another person in yourself". It isn't, however, the same as sympathy. Sympathy is about having an emotional response to someone – but one that isn't shared with them. Empathy's that extra step of thinking 'what is it really like to be the other person with their experiences and their view of the world? How would I feel if I was going through this?

Five Important Empathy Guidelines

- Empathy is expressing what <u>we think</u> we are hearing. On many occasions our thinking may not be clear. Phrases like "<u>that sounds</u> very frustrating" & "<u>that seems</u> so sad" & "<u>that sounds like</u> a horrific loss for you" are very useful as they respectfully allow the speaker to clarify. They are free to agree ("that is exactly how I'm feeling") or disagree ("no, its not really that, I feel more........). Either way the pastoral conversation continues.

- For our empathy statements to sound natural and not artificial the inflection of our voice is very important. It needs to match the emotion you are feeding back.

- Empathy statements do not always express both the emotional & loss component. If the speaker expresses the emotion clearly then generally the empathy statement will focus on the loss. And visa versa. We don't want to sound like a parrot!

- Often the speaker will mention a few losses and emotions. It's best if you feedback just one emotion and/or loss, usually the one you think is most relevant to the speaker at the moment. If it is not the most relevant to the speaker, he/she will probably still mention the most relevant again as the conversation continues. When that happens try to feed back that emotion and/or loss. <u>This process helps the speaker sort out for themselves what they are groaning about. This will not only help the speaker get their groan "off their</u>

chest" but will also help them understand what is going on for them. This will increase their sense of dominion over themselves even thought their circumstances have not changed.

- It's not about getting the "perfect response" (there is no such thing) it's about communicating that not only are you willing to be with them but you are willing to try and understand them. In the end you may not understand the speaker's groan but you have been willing to sit with the speaker as they groan. This we know communicates a great deal.

Marshall Rosenberg, in *Non-Violent Communication: A Language of Life*, states: Empathy requires us to focus full attention on the other person's message. There is a Buddhist saying that aptly describes this: "Don't just do something, stand there". Resist the urge to do something. There are times when just *being there* is more than enough, and at times chaplains may feel the need to add a word or something to a situation. Be intuitive to what is *most needed at a given time*, rather than just saying something so as to feel useful. Again, this is summed up beautifully by Henri Nouwen:

Waiting in another's uncertainty and experiencing something of their loss of control is paradoxically both to inhabit and hold a liminal space where terrible truths are realised and meaning may be glimpsed or remain elusive. What is not required in response are words of explanation or a theological treatise, but an acknowledgement of pain and more waiting. Henri Nouwen (1996, 359) states, "Such waiting is active and never passive.

Expressing Empathy - Being Clear About Emotions

<u>Muddled Expressions for our Emotions</u>

Often in our society when we speak about our emotions, we use expressions that under closer scrutiny are not very clear.

For example, if a person is asked "how are you feeling emotionally?" the following responses would generally be seen as quite acceptable responses. However, on inspection these statements are not expressing clearly a person's emotional state.

Response	What is actually being described by these words?	What a clearer emotional response might look like?
"I'm feeling so tired"	Their physical state	"I'm feeling frustrated because I just don't like being tired"
"I'm feeling really confused"	Their mental state	"I'm actually quite scared as I can't seem to think straight"
"I'm feeling just so lonely"	Their relational state	"When I'm alone that's when I feel the saddest"

"I really feel he is making the wrong decision"	Their opinion about the decision being made by another person	I'm nervous because I don't want him to lose out & I think he will"
"I feel like such an idiot"	Their opinion about themselves	I'm so annoyed, I was wanting to make a good impression & then I said it"

In each one of the above examples, it is most likely the person's body language & the inflection of their voice not their words that will tell us what they are feeling emotionally.

Implications for Pastoral Listening

If we don't speak about emotions clearly then we are not going to able to feedback to others their emotions very clearly. When we can do that, it can help them understand themselves a lot better & it will certainly give them a great sense that we are really listening & seem to understand what they are going through.

Four Emotions

To help us identify the emotions of another (and ourselves) let's say there are just four emotions that people experience. These four will have a whole range of intensity & we have many words to describe them, but in the end there are just four!

Expressing Empathy: Examples

Listener (1)	**How are things going**
Friend	*"Well actually not very well. My house was robbed on Tuesday. Not only did they take what you would expect, camera, some cash that was lying around but for some reason they took a lot of my family photos. I tell you if I had been given half the chance I would have strangled the ratbags. Though at the moment I'm just feeling pretty low because (pause) to be honest I'm even a bit nervous about staying in the house by myself at the moment."*
Listener (2)	**It does sound scary. Your home is meant to be a safe place but at the moment it doesn't seem safe at all!**
Friend	Exactly! …. (pause) The whole thing really has got me down especially being robbed of the photos. The negatives were with them. They can't be replaced.
Listener (3)	**It sounds just so heartbreaking. Those photos are so precious! Now they're gone.**
Friend	Precious. Were they ever! Photos of Great Grandma. All the kids' baby photos. That's why I wanted to

	punch their heads in! I get so angry when I think about it! The scumbags are probably on drugs! What do you think?
Listener (4)	**What do I think? I think you have been robbed of something that is incredibly significant & irreplaceable.**
Friend	Have I ever. .... (long pause) Thanks for listening.
Listener (5)	**Happy to. Is there anything I can do?**
Friend	Not at the moment but I'll give you a ring if there is.

The differences in the responses to the same scenario is stark. One is trying to fix, whilst one is striving to understand. I have had students who have said to me, "We must be careful with our responses because otherwise we will just make things worse". This is not true in my experience. My empathic responses come from a space of love, and therefore I can't make thing worse. If I name the ultimate concern I convey understanding and connectedness, not more suffering. If a child had died due to miscarriage, nothing I will say from a space of love will make that worse. If I say something that comes from a space other than love, then it is possible to make a situation worse. If a chaplain said to a mother who has just had a miscarriage, "Perhaps your smoking has contributed to the loss of your child", then that is not helpful to say the least. I use this fantastic example only to highlight how far a chaplain would have to go to make things worse. A woman shared with me, following her fourth miscarriage, feelings and losses that conveyed to me that this woman would only believe she was a *real* mother if she got to hold her living child in her arms. Before this time, she didn't consider herself a mother yet. I could have challenged that idea, because I believe a pregnant woman is already a mother, however, that would have been about me and not her. Instead, although she had never fully formulated the words, I said to her, "You are so afraid you will never be a mother". This woman looked at me, started crying, and nodding her head. A nurse in the room at the time asked me when I left the room, "Why did you say that to her. You shouldn't have said that, you only made it worse". I replied, "I said what I said because that is how she felt, and nothing I could say could make the death of four children in four pregnancies worse. I named what she was most afraid of and trust me: it helps".

Empathy Exercise - Brett

Bret is someone you get on well with at work. You know that recently his older brother died after a long battle with cancer. On Monday morning when you arrive at work Bret is already at his desk. You say "hi" and ask how his weekend was.

Brett: I just cannot believe it! My brother's ashes were scattered last Thursday afternoon and my parents didn't tell me until I gave them a call over the weekend.

Common Reply: I sure that they just didn't want to bother you knowing how busy you are at the end of the financial year. Its also part of how that generation thinks as well.

1. What do you think is the likely impact of the common reply & why?

_____

_____

_____

_____

_____

2. What seem to be the Brett's losses?

_____

_____

_____

_____

_____

3. What feelings do you think are possibly present? Which one seems to be most clearly expressed at the moment?

_____

_____

_____

_____

4. Write a response that conveys empathy to Brett.

Chapter Six

Identifying and feeding back emotions: Beginning to Understand Emotions

Often in our society when we speak about our emotions, we use expressions that under closer scrutiny are not very clear. When expressing emotions, it is helpful to use words that refer to specific emotions, rather than words that are vague or general. For example, if someone says, "I feel good about that" then the word 'good' could mean many different things: happy, excited, relieved or a number of other emotions. In the appendix I have compiled a list of emotions to help you build on your emotional vocabulary.

For example, if a person is asked "how are you feeling emotionally?" the following responses would generally be seen as quite acceptable responses. However, on inspection these statements are not expressing clearly a person's emotional state.

Response	What is actually being described by these words?	What a clearer emotional response might look like?
"I'm feeling so tired"	Their physical state	"I'm feeling frustrated because I just don't like being tired"

"I'm feeling really confused"	Their mental state	"I'm actually quite scared as I can't seem to think straight"
"I'm feeling just so lonely"	Their relational state	"When I'm alone is when I feel the saddest"
"I really feel he is making the wrong decision"	Their opinion about the decision being made by another person	I'm nervous because I don't want him to lose out & I think he will"
"I feel like such an idiot"	Their opinion about themselves	I'm so annoyed, I was wanting to make a good impression & then I said it"

In each one of the above examples, it is most likely the person's body language & the inflection of their voice not their words that will tell us what they are feeling emotionally.

Implication for Practicing Pastoral Listening

If we don't speak about emotions clearly then we are not going to able to feedback to others their emotions very clearly. When we can do that it can help them understand themselves a lot better and it will certainly give them a great sense that we are really listening and seem to understand what they are going through.

Four Emotions

To help us identify the emotions of another (and ourselves) let's say there are just four emotions that people experience. These four will have a whole range of intensity and we have many words to describe them but in the end, there are just four!

The 'How to'

As I'm listening to a person's story, in the back of my mind I'm wondering, "How would I feel if I was going through this same situation?" With practice, I have been able to access those emotions and losses very quickly, and then I 'feed' that back to the person. For example, a person says, "The doctors have just told me that I have stage 4 cancer of the lungs. I'm not concerned for myself really, I have no choice but to accept it, but I am worried for my wife. We have a disabled son, and now my wife will be all alone caring for him. She needs my help with so many things, but my help won't be available for much longer. It's overwhelming". I then ask myself, "What if I only had a short time to live. How would that feel? How would I feel about leaving my wife alone in this life, especially if we have children we still cared for? I can understand that you may be wondering, "How can you be listening if you have all this self-talk going on?" However, with practice this becomes more and more an unconscious ability, and only takes a second or two. Also, you do not have to start from scratch every time, because as chaplains we hear very similar instances of suffering and tragedy, and so responses become even more natural, spontaneous and can be used again. So, I could respond to the above example, "Crushing to feel like you are leaving your wife to manage everything on her own, and she may not be ready". Now, if the person doesn't agree, they will let you know. For example, they may respond, "I don't feel like its crushing me….I guess for me I feel guilty because I chose to smoke all those years". So, the person 'supervises' our responses, and even if I 'got it wrong' they still feel I'm striving to understand what they are going through.

Empathy Exercise - Pat

Pat is a good friend who you knew was going to see the doctor for what he hoped would be his final all clear visit. You had told him that you would ring up that night and so you did. After saying hello Pat goes on.

Pat-I could kill that doctor. For months he's been telling me everything's fine and now he says it looks like cancer. I've got tests tomorrow, a scan the next day and who know what they'll do to me then!

Common Reply-Look, there's no use getting all worked up. These days they can just about cure almost anything. And what from what I hear Dr Johnson is a mighty good surgeon.

1. What do you think is the likely impact of the common reply & why?

_____

_____

_____

_____

_____

2. What seem to be the Pat's losses?

_____

_____

_____

_____

_____

3. What feelings do you think are possibly present? Which one seems to be most clearly expressed at the moment?

_____

_____

_____

_____

4. Write a response to Pat that conveys empathy.

Practicing Pastoral Listening

Beginning to Understand Emotions

Basic Name	Memory Name	Range of Intensity & Expressions		
Happy	Glad	Little bit… So ……… Very ………	Relieved Encouraged Delighted Elated	"Over the moon"

Angry	Mad	Incredibly …	Frustrated Annoyed Furious Livid	"Steam was coming out of my ears"
Sad	Sad		Discouraged Unhappy Miserable Heartbroken	"Just wanted to cry & cry"
Scared	Bad		Nervous Worried/Anxious Afraid Terrified	"Scared out of my wits"

Beginning to Understand Emotions - Exercise

Part 1 - Identifying the Emotion Exercise

Write down the emotion that you think is being expressed.

1	I can't stand it when he turns up late!!
2	I tell you what, I miss her so much.
3	I don't know, I've got this job, then another, then another, I'm not sure I'm going to cope.
4	I can't stand it when she takes money out of my wallet & doesn't tell me.

Part 2 - Feeding Back the Emotion Exercise

Write down how you might feedback the emotion that is being expressed.

5	I asked him to get the tickets and then he forgets!
6	I was really looking forward to this concert, it would have been great.

7	If this drought continues I'm not sure I'll be able to stay in business.
8	If that waiter had made another mistake, I would have throttled him!
9	Gee, I'm not looking forward to this Driving Test. I hear they have made it a lot tougher.

Beginning to Understand Emotions - Review

Part 1 - Identifying the Emotion Exercise Completed

1	I can't stand it when it when he turns up late!	Angry
2	I tell you what, I miss her so much.	Sad
3	I don't know, I've got this job, then another, then another, I'm not sure I'm going to cope.	Scared
4	I can't stand it when she takes money out of my wallet & doesn't tell me!	Angry

Part 2 - Feeding Back the Emotion

5	I asked him to get the tickets & then he forgets!	That's so annoying!
6	I was really looking forward to this concert, it would have been great.	That's so disappointing!
7	If this drought continues I'm not sure I'll be able to stay in business.	It's a scary time.
8	If that waiter had made another mistake I would have throttled him!	It sounds so frustrating!
9	Gee, I'm not looking forward to this Driving Test, I hear they have made it a lot tougher.	Sounds nerve racking.

Chapter Seven

Expressing Empathy: Seeing all the losses: Beginning to
Understand Losses

<u>Losses are more complex than we think</u>

Sometimes we can be a bit simplistic about the losses that
people experience. We can think that the only factor that
determines one's experience of loss is the associated event. For
example, when we hear that someone has had their Driver Licence
cancelled, we would expect there to be a significant sense of loss
associated with this event. Certainly, we would expect a greater
experience of loss with this event than if the event was the theft of
twenty dollars. Of course, if the event in question was the serious
illness of a loved one then we would expect the sense of loss to be
greater. We develop a sort of grief scale. If event 'A' happens then so
much loss will be experienced. If event 'B' happens then a different
amount of loss is experienced and so on. However, as the table
below shows there are more factors involved in a person's sense of
loss than just the event.

Three People	Same Event	Life Situation	Personal Issues	Sense of Loss
Arthur	Cancellation of Driver Licence	Hardly needs to drive		Very Little

Barry	Cancellation of Driver Licence	Needs licence for employment		Shaken
Cory	Cancellation of Driver Licence	Needs licence for employment	Being able to drive - Significant Identity Issue	Absolutely Devastated

Summary

Event ≠ Loss

Loss = event + life situation + personal issues

Implication for Practicing Pastoral Listening

This complexity of losses challenges us to listen very carefully to the diversity of losses we can experience and speak about. Also, this complexity shows us how dangerous it is for us to think that since I have gone through an event that is similar to another person's event, I now know the losses that this person is now experiencing. Even if we have gone through similar events in our life, who we are as people is different and so our loss experience will be different.

Four Types of Losses

To help us see & hear the complexity of losses that people can experience (including ourselves) let's say there are four general types of losses that people can experience. As with the four basic emotions not only will their intensity vary from one person to another but the number of losses being experienced will also vary.

For example, let's look at Cory who was absolutely devastated when he lost his driving licence.

Functional Losses	Yes	Cory will not be able to get around as easily as he has in the past. This will mean that many basic life events will take longer or not happen at all.
Identity Losses	Yes	Cory is a bit of a "rev head". He has always enjoyed driving & technically can handle a car very well. Not being able to drive is like having a significant part of him removed. It seems to Cory that he is no longer whole.
Relational Losses	Yes	Cory's girlfriend lives a few suburbs away. He will not see her so often. When she does drive them some place they both get very "stressed".
Material Losses	Yes	Cory has to change jobs. His pay is less. He is finding out that Taxis are not cheap.
Functional	Not able to do what you normally can	
Identity	Thoughts/images of myself/world/future no	

	longer seem to be true
Relational	Relationships less than what they were
Material	Loss of possessions, includes financial loss as well

Chapter Eight

Identifying and feeding back the loss

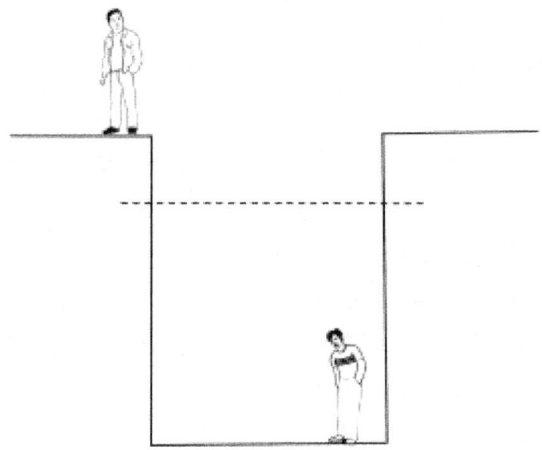

Generally, we think the helpful thing to do when someone mentions a loss is say something positive. We think that if we feedback the loss this will only push the person into a 'pit of despair' or push them further down into their 'pit' and make matters worse. Not so! The person is already in their 'pit'. What you make clear with your positive comment is that *you don't understand them* & most likely you are finding it too uncomfortable to be with them in their 'pit'. You intentionally or unintentionally minimise their sense of loss.

It is only when we feedback their loss, which is often stating how important what they have lost actually is, that the person will for themselves draw upon the internal resources that they already have. Often this means that they will think of some positive perspectives themselves.

<u>Beginning to Understand Losses - Exercise</u>

Wendy is catching up with a friend, Louise, over a cup of coffee. Wendy starts talking about her son James, who is 21, lives at home and according to his mum leads a life full of excesses.

"Why me? Why didn't I have all girls? That son of mine will be the death of me. The other night I get a call from Nepean Hospital at 4am. James has badly smashed two bones in his leg. Apparently, he and his mates were running through some vacant block, God only knows why, and James puts his foot in a hole and that's the end of his leg. Well for the time being anyway. They've had to use those metal rods that go right through his leg and attach them to a big horrible, metal frame. I've seen him every day and I still get shivers up my spine when I see them. You know, when it happened, he was so drunk he didn't feel any pain. I felt so embarrassed when the nurse told me. I don't know! Is he ever going to grow up? He has only just started a new job. Fortunately, they said they're going to keep his job, but they have put him on leave without pay. But he still has other fines to pay so he has asked for another loan. I say "Yes", and you know what he says to me. "Thanks mum" No! He starts telling me how he is missing his mates and that they are not visiting him that much. And to cap it all off you know what he seems to be most upset about? The fact that his favourite tattoo got messed up in the operation. Louise where did I go wrong?!"

Note – For this exercise you will be first imagining that James is groaning directly to you not his mother. Secondly for both James

& Wendy any loss that they mention you will be assuming that it is a major loss even if this story indicates that it may not be. This assumption means that you have to think a feedback comment for each possible loss.

Beginning to Understand Losses – Exercise Summary

	Loss	Loss Type	Some examples of feeding back the loss
James	Broken Leg	Functional	"its such a big loss – being able to get around is so important"
	Tattoo messed up	Identity	"It's like part of you is missing!" or "it really said who you are!"
	Missing his mates	Relational	"you're really out of the loop at the moment" or "life is so much about good friends"

	Only on leave without pay & fines	*Material*	"those fines sound like a bit of a burden" or "when you're strapped for cash you can't buy what you want"
Wendy	Thinking she had failed as mother	Identity	"you have all these hopes & dreams for James but they're not happening"
	Not appreciated by James	Relational	"it would be really nice for James to appreciate you but he doesn't seem to"
	Visiting everyday	Functional	"it really takes a big chunk out of your day"

	Helping James financially	Material	"it sounds like an unexpected drain on your finances"

Chapter Nine

Expressing Empathy: Impact of Feeding Back Losses

For most people saying the above comments goes 'against the grain'. However, when people do feedback these sorts of loss comments the loss is no longer ignored and is in a way *'named'* or acknowledged & out into the open.

The speaker is now in a better position to use the resources that they already have to cope with the losses they are experiencing. Importantly, the listener has also communicated that not only do they seem to understand what the speaker is going through but they are also not afraid to be with them in their 'moment of despair'. This almost unexpected act of love and grace shows how valuable they are.

This encouragement comes at a time when the actions of those around them do not seem to be communicating this to them. One can imagine James thinking that if his mother really loved him she would not expect him to be a person that he is not or Wendy thinking that if James loved me he would not do these sorts of things. In the midst of this the pastoral listener can communicate love to them both.

Empathy Responses-Exercise

Scenario:

1	I've lived in my little house for over 50 years, and now the kids want to put me in a Home. Right now they're clearing out my house. It's all been decided. All my belongings….gone.
2	I am angry! Anyone would be the same! Two weeks turns into seven! My husband is not well and he can't drive, and yet he comes to see me every day. He cannot keep that up much longer. I think we both are reaching the end of our tether.
3	It was four years ago….my daughter….she died of liver cancer. I felt like God was punishing me, but I didn't know why, but that's how I felt…I mean, we were all praying and nothing happened…she died anyway…Its life but…it's so unfair

4	I am really upset this morning, I just heard that one of our staff members, a friend really, passed away through the night. About three weeks ago she had a brain aneurysm and came to hospital, but she died in her sleep overnight.

Scenario responses

Write down how you might respond:

1	
2	
3	
4	

Empathy Exercise - Dianne

Dianne is the daughter of a good friend that you gave known for many years and have gotten on well with. Dianne has been in a long-term relationship that has recently ended. Both of you just happen to meet on the train and after a bit of a chat Dianne says:

My bloody Mum, she keeps asking me to come to her big Christmas party. I just don't feel like celebrating after what I've been through. Everyone will be there with someone except me.

Common Reply-Come on Di, your mum probably just thinks that you'll never get back to normal if you shut yourself away? Anyhow, it's not as if the two of you were married. He was only a boyfriend and there are plenty more out there for a pretty girl like you.

1. What do you think is the likely impact of the common reply and why?

---

2. What seem to be the Dianne's losses?

_____

_____

_____

_____

3. What feelings do you think are possibly present? Which one seems to be most clearly expressed at the moment?

_____

_____

_____

_____

_____

4. Write a response which conveys empathy to Dianne.

_____

_____

_____

_____

_____

Chapter Ten

Example verbatims

Latin has a phrase for "exactly as written": *verbatim ac litteratim,* which literally means "word for word and letter for letter." Like the *verbatim* in that Latin phrase, the English *verbatim* means "word for word." As you may have noticed, there's a *verb* in *verbatim*—and that's no mere coincidence. Both *verb* and *verbatim* are derived from the Latin word for "word," which is *verbum.* Other common English words that share this root include *adverb, proverb,* and *verbose.* Even the word *'word'* itself is related. *Verbatim* can also be an adjective meaning "being in or following the exact words" (as in "a verbatim report") and a rarer noun referring to an account, translation, or report that follows the original word for word.

The verbatim tool is an excellent method of improving what we do as chaplains. It is a record, as best we can recall, of an interaction in time. Like a photo, the verbatim provides the opportunity to sit with and reflect on that particular interaction, now, or at some point in the future. I regularly look at past verbatims and ask myself questions, such as: What are my thoughts and feelings looking at this verbatim today? What, if anything would I say/do differently? How did my responses affect this encounter? How could I have responded differently, and what impact might that have had on the conversation? These and other types of questions allow me one method of continuous improvement. Below, I had added some sample verbatims, in order for you to see the template we use, and so you can see the manner in which I respond. I have deliberately used the verbatims I wrote when I first started in chaplaincy. All the details have been altered to preserve confidentiality and anonymity.

Example layout of a verbatim:

Example Verbatim # 1

Name of trainee: Michael

Date: 3rd January, 2018.

Patients Name: Elisa Smith

Denomination: N/A

Marital status: Widower

Date written: 3rd January, 2018.

Number of previous visits: Nil

Duration of visit: 20 minutes

Background

I had been assigned a ward to visit, and as I entered the ward, the usual concern arose in my mind as I am about to 'Cold Call' on patients. After having 3-4 rejections of my offer for a talk, I came to Elisa. Elisa was in a room with 3 other patients. I always find it easier to go and make my offer of a talk to patients in a single room. Perhaps it is easier to have no audience when my offer is not accepted, and also, when my offer is not accepted, I sometimes feel the other patients in the room think, "Oh no. He is going to ask me!" Elisa appeared to be just sitting and looking out the window when I entered. She turned and looked at me, and I just kept looking at her as I approached her bed. She appeared to be an older lady, slight in build, and with a blank expression.

Aim:

The aim remains the same: work with what a patient offers me, but by using the pastoral care approach, create the possibility that the patient may invite me into the pit they are in, and then to join them in their pit.

The Groan:

C1: Hello, my name is Michael. I am one of the chaplains in the hospital and I am visiting the ward to visit with the patients. Would you like to have a visit today?

P1: Not really…I am waiting for my son to come and see me. It is his birthday, so he is bringing a cake and he is going to take me on a walk around the hospital (big smile)

C2: You look very excited and happy to be seeing him. (At this point I would have walked away, but I did want to acknowledge her smile before I left, but at this response of mine, Elisa continued).

P2: Yes, I am. It's not his birthday today, but I missed it because I was in here. I don't like being in here. Look, they even put the bars up on my bed, and I can't just get up and go to the toilet, but I have to wait for someone to come.

C3: Sometimes this place can feel more like a prison than a hospital

P3: Yes, well it's my own fault I guess…for some unknown reason I fell out of my bed, which has never happened before, and of course I woke up, and instead of pushing this LIFEFORCE pendant I have in order to get help, I just tried to pull myself up on the side of the bed, and when I did I felt this 'CRACK' right across my chest. Then I pressed my pendant and an ambulance arrived and brought me here.

C4: My goodness, life can change so suddenly.

P4: It sure does….anyway, now they want to send me home, but I am not sure if that's the best thing. I don't feel 100% steady when I am on my feet.

C5: It sounds like you're concerned you might not be ready to leave

P5: Exactly…I think I need a bit more time, just to be sure…I don't want to end up in a nursing home…that's not for me…I have lived in my little home for 28 years…my husband built the house, and I feel I would be leaving him if I had to leave the house.

C6: It would feel like you were losing him for the second time

P6: Exactly…Oh, he was such a wonderful man…we had so many plans…he died of a heart attack.

C7: Devastating to lose your husband and all the dreams and plans you both had

P7: It was…he had chest pains at home, so he was taken by ambulance to Mt. Druitt hospital, but there was no doctor 'On-Call' at the time we arrived. We just waited through the night, and at 0530 in the morning, he had a massive heart attack. They took him to another room because it was serious, and then they came and told me he was gone (starts crying).

C8: That's so terribly sad Elisa, it must have seemed like a bad dream, so shocking.

P8: I was in shock at first, but then I was angry that no doctor was available, and now I wonder would my husband had lived if there was a doctor…you know

C9: So heartbreaking to think that he may have survived if help was available

P9: Yes…my son too, has regrets…he was going to come to the hospital early that morning before work, but decided he would see his father in the afternoon after work, but of course his father was gone. He has a terrible regret.

C10: It sounds like he is haunted by the missed opportunity to see his dad.

P10: He can't forget it…Why do you think God took my husband, I mean, he was such a good man

C11: It seems like you are really struggling to understand why God allows some things to happen

P11: (Nodding) (silence)…You know…(starts crying again)…I lost my first baby….I carried her right up until 2 weeks before she was due, and somehow, the cord got caught around her neck…I felt something was wrong, I felt it…but the doctor said she was dead.

C12: Oh Elisa that is so distressing, losing your beautiful baby so close to her birth.

P12: She was my first...and I didn't have her for 4 or 5 months...it was right up to near the birth

C13: So she was already a much-loved part of the family, and you would have had so many hopes and dreams for her.

P13: Yes, her name was going to be Bernadette Rose

C14: Beautiful...what a deep wound to your heart.

P14: (Nodding) Yes...some people said "You will get over it", "Just give it some time", (silence and crying)

C15: I think there are some very painful wounds we never get over, no matter how much time passes.

P15: (silence but shaking her head) Why does God give a child and then take them away!

C16: It's so hard to understand.

P16: He asks us to have children, right? Then He takes them away! I prayed for a miracle when the doctor told me, but it was true, she was gone before she was even born. How is that fair?

C17: Heaven seemed deaf to your prayers, and you lost your precious little girl.

P17: Yes, I lost her, but I will find her again won't I? That's the promise isn't it? We all get to be reunited again, right? All in the kingdom of God, if we are good?

C18: Elisa, He told us, "Do not let your hearts be troubled. You believe in God; believe in Me as well. In My Father's house are many rooms". So yes Elisa, I do believe you will be reunited with your little precious one.

P18: I believe it too…He has looked after me on so many occasions, like sending you here today… you have made my day…it was really lovely meeting you.

C:19: I really thank you for sharing your story with me Elisa. Would you like to finish with a prayer?

P19: Yes, thank you

C20: Do have a special prayer you like to say or would like me to say?

P20: Could you say one?

C21: Heavenly Father, I thank you for the opportunity to meet and spend time with Elisa. I ask that you bless her and send your Grace upon her. I ask that you send your healing spirit upon Elisa, and assist her with a speedy recovery, and soothe the pains in her heart. We know that you understand our doubts and questions, and like a loving Father, you hold us close to you the more we are hurt and suffering. May your Word remind us that life is short, and then forever in your Kingdom of Light we shall rejoice with our families and the saints who have done your Will. We ask your blessings on Elisa's son, whose birthday has just passed, and ask your loving presence for each of the patients in our hospital. We ask all this in the name of Jesus the Lord. Amen.

Verbatim # 2

Name of trainee: Michael

Date: 2nd February, 2018.

Patients Name: Fred Smith

Denomination: Christian

Marital status: Married

Date written: 2nd February, 2018.

Number of previous visits: 1

Duration of visit: 20 min

Background

I had visited Fred about a fortnight earlier, and we had spent about 20 minutes in Fred sharing the story of his life's work: driving buses. I had just planned to say "G'day" to Fred as I had spoken to him before, and there were other new patients in this ward. When I paused to say "G'day" I noticed he looked worried.

Aim:

Just to stop and say, "Hi" to Fred as I passed his room.

The Groan

C1: Hi Fred, I was just visiting the ward, and I thought I would just say "G'day" on my way past.

P1: Oh, G'day mate, what was your name again, I've forgotten, sorry?

C2: It's 'Michael". Are you Ok? You look like you have something on your mind.

P2: Have you got 5 minutes?

C3: Sure Fred (I take a seat).

P3: I got some bad news today. You probably remember that I was hoping to go home a few days after we last spoke, but then the doctors said they were too concerned about me to let me go home. They think my balance is not what it should be. They want me to go to a nursing home, and I said, "Well, then I want to go to the Home my wife is in". You see I have been visiting her very regularly since she has been there, and even though there is staff, I still do a lot for her. I have just found out today I have to go to another Home, so I won't be in the same Home as my wife. There are no rooms available where my wife is.

C4: So distressing to be separated from your wife, and such a feeling of powerlessness to remedy this decision.

P4: Yes, that's right. Looking after her has been a big part of my life for the last 4 years. The doctors say they can get my wife into the Home I am going to, but I don't want to pull her out of a place she has friends and where she has settled into for so long, just to be with me. She even looks after some of the older residents.

C5: It sounds like your wife's happiness comes first, even if it means that you suffer.

P5: True. My wife has dementia, and I looked after her as long as I could. We have been together for 64 years, but it got to the stage where she was doing odd things, like leaving all the hot plates on, and then she would go and watch the telly. I had to constantly be thinking "Where is she, and what is she doing"? Even putting my dirty underwear back in my drawer, things like that. I had to make sure she didn't just walk off and wander down the street.

C6: That sounds very exhausting, and so painful to watch someone we love become so childlike.

P6: It was really hard, so hard. When my own health started to decline, I had to put her in a Nursing Home. It was so hard because she didn't think anything was wrong with her. One of the hardest thing I ever did was put her in a Home, but it had to be done.

C7: Enough to break your heart, Fred.

P7: Too right! Now, I have to get my son to sell my house, and car, and there are things in the house that have family value, but I can't do it. I can barely stand on my own, let alone pack up and sell a house. We lived in the house nearly 35 years. There is a lot of crap and stuff in that house as well. I can't take everything, and I have to leave it up to him, but anyway what can you do?

C8: It's hard to let someone else dispose of our little treasures

P8: It is. Well, you know, they are part of you, the little things we gather through life, and then the time comes when you have to just let them all go

C9: It sounds like you have reached the time when borrowed things must be returned

P9: I never thought of it like that but, yes. You come into the world with nothing and you leave with nothing. It never dawns on you when you are busy collecting stuff, that one day you lose it all anyhow.

C10: And now another loss with being separated from the wife

P10: (silence) I just hope that a room becomes available at her Home sooner rather than later. They won't let me drive anymore, so I have to wait for one of the kids to drive mum to my Home or me to mum's Home, and they are flat out with their own lives, so until we live in the same Home, it will be won't be often, I fear.

C11: The kids don't seem to understand how much you both need each other

P11: (Nodding)… They're just so busy with their own families, kids sport, work, you know, life. I was visiting her nearly every day, and I have been in here nearly four weeks, and my son has only once brought my wife to see me here. And when I thought I was going home, and was going to resume visiting her every day, I find out that I can no longer drive, and I have to go into my own nursing home.

C12: Life seems like one loss after another at the moment

P12: It sure does. I did have plans, and they have to keep changing. Well, at 80 I guess these things happen. Things change, and you have to change with them. With any luck, it will be a short time to when we are both living in the same Home.

C13: It sounds like you still have hope about the future

P13: Yes, I do. I am glad you were able to stop by. Thanks.

C14: You're welcome, Fred. Would you like a prayer before I leave?

P14: Umm..If you would like

C15: Would you like, Fred?

P15: Not really, thanks. But would you keep me in your prayers?

C16: Certainly. God bless.

Verbatim # 3

Name of trainee: Michael

Date: 28th February, 2018.

Patients Name: Ronald Smith

Denomination: Agnostic/Atheist

Marital status: Married

Date written: 28th February, 2018.

Number of previous visits: Nil

Duration of visit: 15 minutes

Background

Ronald was a slim man, who appeared older than his age of 63. He looked bright-eyed and sitting up watching TV. He was showered and dressed, like he was leaving the hospital.

Aim:

Work with what the patient gives me.

The Groan:

C1: Hello, my name is Michael. I am one of the chaplains in the hospital and I am visiting the ward to spend time with patients who may like a visit. Would you like that today?

The Groan:

P1: Yes, that would be ok. What shall we talk about?

C2: Do you feel like sharing what's important to you.

P2: Okay, let's talk about my grandkids, they're coming to visit me anytime now. I know you are a chaplain, but I'm not religious, and in fact I am a bit of an atheist.

C3: You're a bit of an atheist? What's the rest of you then? (Smiling)

P3: A doubter I reckon…I mean how anyone in the world can believe in God if they turn on the TV. All the religions are the same, out for what they can get. My father always said, "I will decide when the believers can agree". All the problems in our world stem from religion. I mean, history is full of the terrible things that we have done to each other in the Name of God. Nah, I don't believe.

C4: It sounds like you're very certain

P4: Yeah… Nah, it can't be right…Well I will know soon enough, won't I…I have cancer in my bones, and the doctor's think I have maybe 6 months.

C5: So, death is right around the corner

P5: Yes, I guess it is. I am not afraid of death, not worried about me, but I am hoping I won't be in too much pain. It hurts to walk around for any length of time, and breathing becomes difficult if I exert myself. But I am more concerned about who is going to take care of things when I am gone, like my wife, she is older, and I have a disabled son, and....anyway lots of things to think about when you're dying

C6: It sounds like you can't even die in peace

P6: (laughs) Yep, so it seems. I looked after everything for years, but now (eye's get watery) ...I can't do it anymore. I even used to work part-time at our local club, but that's finished now. My wife will just somehow have to cope with doing the things I used to take care of.

C7: You're very worried how she is going to manage

P7: Yes, but there is nothing I can do...I can't change what's happening!

C8: It's painful to feel so powerless when it comes to wanting to protect your family

P8: Very true. I always thought it would be better if she went before me, I probably shouldn't say that, but you know what I mean.

C9: You didn't want to leave her alone and facing it all by herself

P9: Yes, that's what I mean... Anyway life had other plans...it always seems too doesn't it?

C10: It seems to be true that very often our plans don't work out the way we imagined

P10: Certainly…you think something is going to happen, and then WAM! Something happens to change everything.

C11: Yes, life can change so suddenly

P11: Like this cancer…that's a big WAM!

C12: Yes, that must have been unexpected

P12: Not really, I mean, it was, but also I have smoked for years, so I sorta thought it might lead to something. So, I guess I deserve this to some extent, I mean smokers have been told for years to quit, and I finally did, but too late in the end.

C13: It sounds like you're blaming yourself for what your family now has to go through

P13: Well, sometimes I think it's my fault. I always knew I could get cancer as a smoker, but the doctor thinks the two things could be unrelated. But who knows for sure. That doesn't really matter now, does it?

C14: No, it doesn't

P14: That's the hard truth. I can hear my Grandkids coming

(Grandkids arrive).

C15: Thanks for the talk

P15: Yeah, thanks for dropping by.

<u>Verbatim # 4</u>

Name of trainee: Michael

Date: 9th March, 2018.

Patients Name: June Smith

Denomination: Anglican

Marital status: Married

Date written: 9th March, 2018.

Number of previous visits: Nil

Duration of visit: 20 minutes

Background

When I entered June's room, she appeared frail and tired. She looked miserable. June was nearly 70 years old according to my paperwork. June has been in hospital much longer than she was told or imagined. Different issues keep arising which means her stay at hospital has been extended. She is concerned for her husband, and the impact her extended stay is having on him. She also received some bad news regarding her health, which June believes is unfair.

<u>Aim:</u>

To work with what a patient gives me and provide comfort via the pastoral care approach.

<u>The Groan:</u>

C1: Hello, my name is Michael. I am one of the chaplains in the hospital and I am visiting the ward to spend some time with patients who may like a visit. Would you like that today?

P1: Okay, but I won't be good company because I am not in a good space right now, I just want to go home, but I seem to be stuck here and nothing seems to be getting any better.

C2: It sounds like you're stuck here

P2: It sure does…Two weeks I was told, and it's been nearly seven!

C3: No wonder you sound angry. Big difference between 2 weeks and seven!

P3: I am angry! Anyone would be the same. My husband is not well, and he can't drive, and yet he comes to see me every day. He cannot keep that up much longer. I think we both are reaching the end of our tether.

C4: It sounds like you just want this resolved so you can get back to your life together.

P4: Yes! Two weeks, that's all they said it would be, and now, the doctor told me I might have emphysema. I have never smoked a day in my life, and now, I have a small pressure sore on my backside that won't heal.

C5: Just feels like things are going from bad to worse

P5: That's it exactly! (Starts to cry). I want to go home, but there are these hurdles that keep coming up to stop me…

C6: Hmmm…(silence, nodding)

P6: And the staff just ignore me. They keep hiding the buzzer...my feet feel like they're on fire and itchy, and I have to scream for help, and when they finally come, it takes them another 15 minutes to get what they need and come back

C7: That must be like torture. We wouldn't treat an animal that way

P7: That's right, we wouldn't. Why but? I don't know what for, I have always minded my own business, and never did anything to anyone...I am a good woman. I felt this way before... I felt punished by God when my daughter died (Crying)

C8: Oh June, your poor wounded heart

P8: It was four years ago....she died of liver cancer...I felt like God was punishing me, but I didn't know why, but that's how I felt...I mean, we were all praying and nothing happened...she died anyway...Its life but...it's so unfair

C9: And now it seems like God is punishing you again

P9: (Crying and nodding) Why is He punishing me, or if He is not punishing me, why doesn't He help me? (Sounding angry)

C10: June, it sounds like you're angry because your experience is not matching your faith

P10: No, it isn't. He supposed to be loving and kind, right? Well, none of my prayers are answered. I don't even pray anymore. What's the point? Might as well tell the wall, it does that much good.

C11: It seems like Heaven is ignoring you, and you don't know what to believe anymore

P11: That's right! (Starts crying) I feel like He has forgotten me, and that I will never get out of here. I just want to go home and be happy and normal with my husband. Is that too much to ask of Him?

C12: No it's not

P12: At least you understand, and I am not sure God does

C13: June, I believe in a Father who loves us, but I struggle at times to see where He is in people's lives

P13: So, you don't understand either? And you're a chaplain?

(Doctor comes in, and asks if he should come back)

P14: No, I need to see you about my feet and the itch.

C14: You're right June, even chaplains can't explain everything. Thank you for sharing June.

P15: Thanks for coming.

Verbatim # 5

Name of trainee: Michael

Date: 2nd March, 2018.

Patients Name: Elaine Smith

Denomination: Anglican

Marital status: Widow

Date written: 2nd March, 2018.

Number of previous visits: 0
Duration of visit: 25minutes

Background:

I received a pager from the NUM of a particular ward at 4pm on a Friday afternoon. At first I was thinking, "Oh, great. Someone waits till Friday afternoon before they realise they want to see a chaplain". I called the ward, and the NUM stated, "I have a lady who would like to see a Protestant minister. Is that something you can organise?" I replied, "Well, there are 1000's of Protestant denominations, so it would help to know what denomination the patient is. Do you happen to know?" The NUM replied, "No, I am not sure". I replied, "How about I come to the ward and speak with the patient, and we will take it from there?" I acknowledge I was a bit "short" with the NUM, as I felt irritated with this late call.

When I arrived at the ward, I introduced myself to the NUM, and got the patients details and room/bed number. When I entered the room, it was darkly lit with window curtains drawn tightly, and I observed an elderly woman who was lying in bed with her fore-arm across her eyes. The ward I was in is quite bright, with loads of natural light, but this room was the opposite: dark and shadowy room, with a lonely figure laying on the flat bed. It seemed a tomb.

Aim:

To facilitate spiritual comfort by collecting enough information for me to find a protestant minister a.s.a.p. given it was Friday 4pm+

The Groan:

C1: Hello, my name is Michael. I am one of the chaplains in the hospital and I received a call from one of the staff of this ward stating that you would like to see a chaplain.

P1: Yes, I want to see someone. What denomination are you?

C2: I am a Catholic

P2: Oh, that's alright, you will do for now, but I would like to see an Anglican Minister.

C3: I can try to organise that for you.

P3: I'm in a terrible way now. I came into the hospital and the doctor took me off all my medications, and put me on something new. That may be good for my body, but my depression had become a lot worse. It's the worst it's been. I haven't felt this depressed since I lost my husband. I am all alone. I lost him about four years ago, and he was the love of my life. We were married for 55 years. It was terrible to lose someone you have been with since you were 25 years old. No one is visiting me, none of my friends or family. I have a son who has a brain injury, and needs looking after, and another son who was born with a brain abnormality, so they can't visit, and I suffer terribly with pain in my body, especially my legs, and now I am so depressed. My husband would have been here to support me but he died, and my only sister died two years ago. Did you want to ask me any questions?

C4: I can't think of any questions to ask you that would help me understand any better than you already have, just how much you have suffered these last few years.

P4: (starts crying) Thank you, thank you…I have suffered so much. I have been in the hospital for nine days, and no one has come to see me, and the staff don't seem to care about anything but my body. And I am so depressed, and they don't seem to notice it.

C5: The first thing I noticed was the darkness of this room, and it seems the darkness in this room is a good reflection of how your life feels right now

P5: Very true. I am so glad that you came to see me. You're a good man, I can tell. My husband was a good man. He was a plumber. He worked very hard, and on top of all that, he went back to school part-time for 11 years and completed a Degree in Engineering. I was so proud of him, but it was hard. He worked 6 days a week and then on Sunday he would do his studies. Me and the kids missed out a lot during those 11 years, but it was worth it in the end, because he was able to work a less physical job, and earn more money.

C6: A tremendous sacrifice for the whole family.

P6: It was a sacrifice. I was lonely for a companion, because he did not have much spare time during those 11 years. Honestly, he wasn't much a companion anyway as far as that goes. I want to tell you something… it's not easy, but I feel I can tell you….that I had a number of affairs on my husband. My husband said, that as far as he could remember, his mother never hugged him or kissed him, and so I think that meant he found it difficult to be affectionate or intimate with me. He found out about one of my affairs. He was devastated. We stayed together, but he never forgave me. I think we stayed together to look after our boys. I regret those mistakes, but at the time I was needing something my husband was unable to give me.

C7: When you are starving you have to eat something.

P7: Yes, that's what it was! I was starved of his attention and affection. I know you just said what you said, you're very kind, but I know as a chaplain you must not approve of my affairs. Looking back now, I wish things could have been different, but I was very lonely. As well, looking after my son who was born with brain damage was such a strain. He needed constant looking after, and I had another son, who was normal, to look after too. Because my disabled son took a lot of my focus, my other son and I grew apart as he got older. He learnt to rely on himself more and more. In a way he missed out on having a good relationship with either of us. When he was 21 he left home, but not long after, he had a car crash and was nearly killed. He ended up with a major brain injury, and needs 24 hr care in a nursing home.

C8: Another terrible blow to your wounded heart

P8: (crying and nodding) I think if it wasn't for my faith, I would not be here today. You would know how important faith is and how we should pray every day. The Lord has certainly tested me, and I haven't always come through with flying colours, so to speak. But I have tried, I have, but I think sometimes, it's been too much. I have had to cope with so many disappointments and failures, and now God is testing me again by being in hospital.

C9: It sounds like you have been through enough trials and tests, and the Lord should pick on someone else

P9: Yes, I can't take any more of this suffering.

C10: It certainly sounds like you are completely worn out right now

P10: That's how I feel. I feel like I'm being punished for all the things I did wrong. I just want to feel better, happier, and get out of here. I hate it here! People just keep coming in and telling me, "You have to do this", "It's time for this", "We just have to do this, now", and I can't get any rest, and I can't eat the food, and it's just awful. My friends in the nursing home can't visit me, and I can't see my boys. I've had enough of this place.

C11: This is Hell for you

P11: Exactly! You are the only one who seems to understand that. None of the staff, or doctors seem to care. They walk in, say something, and walk out. Why has it taken nine days for you to come and see me if you work in the hospital every day? Aren't the chaplains supposed to visit all the patients?

C12: It must seem like everyone, including God and the chaplains have been ignoring you?

P12: I'm sorry. I didn't mean that. I don't mean to sound angry, I am just really grateful you came to see me, and I wish that had happened earlier. Will you come back and see me again. I feel so much better for your visit. You promise to come back?

C13: Of course. I am back in the hospital on Monday, and I will be happy to come and see you. Would you still like me to organise an Anglican minister to come and see you?

P13: No, I don't think I need that after all.

C14: Okay. Would you like me to say a prayer before I leave?

P14: Yes, I was going to ask. Could you say a manly prayer?

C15: Of course.

Heavenly Father, we know you are never far from us, but there are times we feel that you have abandoned us. We feel like we are stuck in so deep a hole that our sighs and tears cannot be heard by You. Come Father, delay no longer. Show us your kindness and let us feel your presence and love. Without You life is a dark hellish prison, and we begin to doubt your Love. Forgive our failings and help us forgive those who have hurt us. Let your beautiful smile arise in our hearts and may we wait for you in joyful expectation for the day in which you call us out of the death of this life and into the true Life with you in your Kingdom. Give us peace here Lord until that time, and bless us all, especially Elaine and her sons, and may your Spirit give them the peace that the world does not know. We ask this Father with great confidence in the name of Jesus our Lord. Amen.

P15: That was beautiful, thank you. God bless you. And remember to come and see me on Monday.

C16: I shall, I promise. God bless you.

P16: Michael...do you mind drawing the curtains a little (smiling)

C17: Gladly.

Student Verbatims and feedback

Pastoral Verbatim Report- example student verbatim #1

Name of Trainee: Gregory

Date: 17/10/22

Patients Name: Julie

Duration of Visit: 40min

Background:

Julie is 37 years old. She is a single parent to her son who is 14 years old. They live with her parents. She is currently in a relationship. She is being treated for cancer.

<u>Aim</u>: To be with the patient and respond to what they offer me.

<u>The Groan:</u>

C1: Hello. My name is Gregory. I am a chaplain here at the hospital and I am going around the ward today visiting patients and was wondering if you would like a visit?

P1: Yea sure!

(I pull a chair over and sit down. Julie is sitting up in a chair in casual clothes not a hospital gown).

C2: What is your name?

P2: Julie

C3: It's nice to meet you, Julie. How long have you been here for?

P3: Forty-five days. See, on the white board over there I'm keeping count.

C4: Gosh that's a big chunk of time.

P4: Yep. I was told forty-five days ago that I have cancer.

C5: That is very confronting news to hear

P6: It was a shock because you never think it's going to be you. I spent eleven days in the ICU which was absolutely terrible! It was a really scary time, not knowing really what was happening to me and what was going to happen. I was in so much pain, feeling like I just want to die but at the same time live because I have a son. The pain was unbearable at times.

(Julie talked more about the physical and mental difficulties she has experienced through this time)

C7: It sounds like a very traumatic experience.

P7: It definitely has been, in lots of different ways, ways you wouldn't even think about. They actually have been treating me with arsenic. Which was a shock! Initially I would experience headaches like I never imagined possible, like I felt my head was going to explode. There was also dryness of mouth, loss of taste and other stuff. It's been crazy and there really wasn't much they could do to help all the side effects. Now when they give it to me, I don't experience much of that anymore which makes me worry that my body is used to this chemical.

C8: How horrible for you

P9: My family has been amazing. Mum and dad would come and sit with me, even if I was asleep the whole time. Mum is looking after my son. It's hard on her though because she works as well, and she also wants to be visiting me and she's doing my washing. It's a lot for her, but the wider family has really stepped up too, making meals and stuff. (Julie talked more about her family and friends)

C9: Its sounds like you have great support system

P10: I think it's one of the big reasons I have gotten through this. But it's also been hard dealing with people's positivity through it, people trying to encourage you and make you feel better, when I'm not always feeling that way. Sometimes you just want to be able to say how you are feeling and not have someone try and say something positive back at you. Instead, you just want them to agree with you. You know someone will send a super long, super positive text and I'm not necessarily thinking "yay", but I have noticed that after the fact those messages really have helped me.

C11: It seems like a real up and down journey emotionally for you

P12: More than you can even imagine. The hardest part has been watching my son through it all. I can see it affecting him. I'm a single mum, it's just me and him so much of the time. So having my Mum looking after him instead of me is really different for him. The good thing is we do live with my parents, so he's got the stability of the same living arrangement. He loves my mum of course it's just different.

C12: It must be hard for you not being able to do the things you usually do for him.

P13: Absolutely! it's just another thing you have to adjust to. So many things. But you know, we try and make the most of the time when he's here, watching movies, playing games, just hanging out depending on how I'm going.

I might actually be going home at the end of this week. I'm having some tests done then the doctors will make a decision. The next stage is two weeks at home and then after that for quite some time I come in here Monday to Friday for 4hours each day to be treated again. Weirdly, it's scary the thought of being at home now even though I want to go. I had a few hours recently out of the hospital and nearly had a panic attack. Not having the nurses and doctors

around checking everything is ok was unnerving, as well as being around other people because my immunity is compromised.

C13: It seems like hospital has become a safe place for you

P14: I had no idea until I had left the hospital! I've been reading up a lot on other people's experiences. It's been helpful to see how others have moved ahead through this journey, especially the things I hadn't thought about that I might face. It's still hard though, so much unknown but I guess not as much as before! It has really changed the way I look at life now. Things that I used to see as important just don't seem that important now. Things I used to worry about just seem silly now. Things that I appreciate now that I took for granted (she talked about this for a bit)

C14: This has given you a different lens to look through, a new perspective.

P15: It has in a good way I think.

(We chatted for a little more about lighter stuff)

C15: It's been a privilege to hear your story. I will be praying for you during the week

P16: Thank you, it's been helpful to talk with someone totally separate from it all.

Response to student verbatim #1

- C1: Good intro. Clear, respectful and with choice or refusal offered
- C3: Not too bad, but for me, your question sets the direction of the conversation, i.e. duration of stay. Like you, when I sit down after being invited, I will ask, "What would you like to talk about?" They may say, "Oh I don't know, what about you?". I will reply, "Why don't you tell me what's most important to you right now". Anyway, a small matter, I guess, but it leaves them free to direct the sharing. Duration really is not too important: a week/month it's all an interruption to their life. Unless they mention 'time' I typically don't.
- C5: ok
- C7: good

- C8: good
- C9: ok
- C11: ok. Interesting to note her comments about others trying to give a positive or hopeful spin on her situation. You see it really doesn't help, so it's vital we as chaplains don't do this. They don't need us to, as everyone else in their life is already doing that, in order to make the person and themselves feel better.
- C12: ok. Try and find another word for 'hard'- sad, painful, disappointing, unfair, frustrating, etc
- C13: very good response. Nailed it!
- C14: good

I thought you handled this encounter really well. It was a deep 'pit' for this young woman to deal with, and you were able to feedback empathic statements which enabled Julie to continue sharing. I noticed through the verbatim that Julie said a lot, and then you made a short statement. This is the way to keep the focus on the other and off us. I'm not sure how you were feeling throughout this encounter, but from reading the verbatim I was not detecting any undue stress or anxiety on your behalf. You sounded relaxed and attentive. You contained your fixes, your curiosity, your advice, your shared experiences, etc. Well done. Keep reflecting on your practice and start journaling if you haven't already. In a few months, look at this verbatim again, and see if you can come up with other responses, and imagine how that may have affected the conversation.

Pastoral Verbatim Report- example student verbatim #2

Date: 10th August 2021

Person name: Kerry

Married with 2 children

Date written: 12th August 2022

Duration of chat 45 minutes

Background:

Kerry is a friend who is having marriage problems and rang upset one night. We organised a day to meet as she was very overwhelmed with what to do.

Aim:

Checking that Kerry is OK and listen to what she wanted to share. She said that she needed to talk so that she can work out what is going on and what to do.

The Groan:

C1- Hi hon.

P1-Thanks for meeting with me. I am so frustrated and confused as Pete is so angry and I cannot talk to him. I really don't know what to do!

C2- I'm here for you

P2- I know thanks. I am just so worried about him as he seems so agitated, but he won't talk to me about what's wrong. And the kids are becoming anxious too.

C3- so upsetting for you and worrying for the kids too

P3- I just wanted to share with someone and hopefully it will help me to calm down and work out what to do as I am totally lost.

C4: talk to me

P4- Reggy comes home every night for the past 2 weeks agitated and won't talk to me. He will chat with the kids, but he tends to leave after dinner and comes home after I have gone to bed. I don't know if it is about work or me or something else?

C5- how awkward for you

P5- I thought that if I just shared what was going on it would help me but maybe I should talk to a counsellor or helpline or someone.. I want to be able to help him but he won't let me.

C6: How are you going?

P6-Well, I am very hurt obviously but to be honest I am starting to get angry with him and then I am taking it out on the kids as I am so frustrated and that is not what I want to happen at all.

C7: Hard not to get angry when hurt

P7-Yeh it is but what else can I do

We spoke a bit more and she decided when a bit calmer to let Reggy know that if he didn't talk to her about what's wrong then she will involve the family as it was starting to hurt the children and she was getting very agitated and upset every day.

She spoke to her husband after we spoke and says While she understood he was in a bad place maybe he needed help to work it out. He accepted that he had been acting badly and agreed that they both sit down with someone to talk about how he was feeling and why. This has not happened yet but the situation has improved slightly due to starting to communicate with each other again.

As for my part I found it difficult not to jump in and give advice or suggestions, but I did find that by just listening to Kerry she was able to share all she needed to without my commenting much.

Jackie

Feedback to student verbatim #2

Hi Jackie,

I felt reading this that you were struggling with your responses.

- In response to P1, you replied "I'm here for you". That is obvious by your presence. Another response was called for, for e.g. "It sounds like a really scary situation". Again, silence with some head nodding and a little 'sound' (Hmm..) from you would have been better and given Kerry 'permission' to continue.
- C3: was better, but close to parroting. Instead, something like, "Whatever is going on is effecting the whole family badly" OR, "He doesn't seem himself, and that's scary".
- C4: "talk to me". She is, but she is not feeling the connection between you both. Another response to P3 like, "It sounds like you're in a very dark place at the moment".

- C5: "How awkward for you". No Jackie, Kerry is not feeling awkward, she is feeling scared, confused, hurt, angry, a sense of impending doom, but not awkward. You are feeling awkward. You're not sure how to respond to this. You are struggling to put yourself in Kerry's shoes to imagine what it would be like if your husband behaved this way. So, one response could be, "It seems like a million miles between you both, and whatever is going on is not good". or, "It seems like the family is falling apart and he doesn't want to talk about it". or "He's behaviour is really scarring you and it's like you're not even there". You see Jackie, you are trying to imagine how Kerry feels, and then Kerry will guide you about how close you are to what she is feeling. Whether you're too strong or not, for example, she may say, "Oh, I don't think the family is falling apart, it's just beyond strange the way he is behaving", or she might say, "Yes, that's what I'm afraid of. I don't want to lose my family". Kerry will be your guide: you just follow.

- P5: Kerry tells you that you are not getting it, that's why she states she needs to talk to someone.... anyone else. You respond, "How are you going?" To me this is a clear sign that your head is spinning. You're not sure what to say, and so you say what you said. It's a throw away response. Better to remain silent. A response to P5, could have been, "It sounds like you're feeling so helpless in this situation" OR, "It sounds like you need some answers about where to go from here". Now, I won't provide any answers, but I demonstrate that I'm listening. If she wants answers, then let her seek them at a counsellors or helpline. We listen and empathise, not solve or fix. Kerry can't even fix this because right now, "He won't let me".

- P6, she sounds a bit frustrated with you: "Well, I am very hurt obviously".
- C7: Try not to use the word, 'hard', and close to parroting again. Another response could have been, "It sounds like the whole family is suffering through this". or, "It's very easy when you're on tenterhooks to snap at anyone and anything".

Jackie, it wasn't all bad, because you're right, it would have been very easy in this relationship to offer advice, which you didn't. That was excellent, because it would have been tempting, given Kerry is looking for answers or help. Remember, practice trying to imagine you are in the shoes of the person talking and imagine what feelings would come up for you. Keep it simple: Mad, Bad, Sad, Glad. This story was Mad (she was getting angry because she was fearful and scared), Bad, and sad. So, work those words or similar into your responses. Practice re-writing this verbatim with some different responses. Ask yourself: What was going on for me during this encounter? How was I feeling? What could I have done differently?

Pastoral Verbatim Report- example student verbatim #3

Student: Richard

Date: 17th September 2021.

Name of person: Ian

Date written: 18th September, 2021.

Duration: 15 minutes

Background:

I had the opportunity to visit a friend who unexpectantly ended up in hospital a few days earlier following a medical situation. The intention of the visit was primarily as a friend, however I intended to be alert for any opportunity for pastoral intervention, but I certainly didn't want to "force it". Walking into the ward I noticed many drawn curtains, a few open with patients present. Some unmade beds and the occasional stripped bed. Entering the room Ian looked thin, tired, and a bit drawn. None the less he greeted me happily.

After some general chit chat and catching up, **I attempted to draw the conversation in a pastoral direction.** The opening dialogue is below.

Aim: To gain practical experience in pastoral care, as well as visiting a friend.

The Groan:

C1: So how have you been finding it here?

P1: Oh, the worst thing was the wait in the waiting room for nine hours.

Richard did mention he has been a bit anxious but was relieved some initial tests and procedures are over for now. Unfortunately, the conversation quickly became general chat again about medical tests just done, and future treatment. I was having difficulty thinking how to draw the conversation back to something pastoral without feeling it was going to sound and seem forced and weird. At this point I had mixed emotions with a bit of disappointment, although I was happy to see my friend, I was mentally resorting to my alternative plans to gaining practice elsewhere.

To my surprise, as it was coming up to the end of visiting hours and I was beginning to make moves to leave, Jerry mentioned an experience he had shortly before coming to hospital. It occurred whilst he had a high fever, and whilst the explanation may simply be medical, it affected him not only emotionally, but also spiritually.

The beginning of this part of our conversation is below:

P2: I've never told anyone this before, but the other day I had a nightmare.

Richard began to explain several days ago (before hospitalisation) he had a very high fever and had a nightmare. He had a physical sensation that affected him not only physically, but it had distressed him both emotionally and spiritually. I could clearly see in his eyes this was still causing him some fear and distress. At this point my heart went out to him and I wanted to help him through this. To me it was an unexpected need for pastoral care. An extract of the dialogue continues below.

C2: That must have been terrifying. How did you handle it?

P:3 I prayed.

C3: So, you handled it with prayer?

C4: Were you feeling distressed?

P4: Not really. It didn't last long. I'm sure it was just a dream.

C5: How about we pray with you now?

P5: Richard nodded and closed his eyes ready for prayer.

After a short prayer I left Richard. He seemed calm and more at peace. He also seemed grateful for the support.

<u>My response and feedback</u>

Your comment in the 'Background':

- David, despite what you meant, as a rule we allow the patient/friend to lead the conversation. I for one never attempt to draw a conversation in a pastoral direction, but I am always at the ready to follow wherever the person leads me. If they lead me into a boring social chat about stamp collecting, I go. If they lead me into a dark disgusting pit, I go. It's always up to them. If they lead me into the pit and then want to jump straight out for whatever reason, then I jump out with them. It's up to them.

- At C2: David, your initial statement is ok, but you followed it up with a question. One of the things I want you to learn, is when the conversation changes from social to pastoral, in nearly every case, <u>you stop</u>

<u>asking questions</u>. You see, you asked him a feeling question followed by a 'head' question. You didn't need to ask him, "How did you handle that?". He would have told you without the question. Even, "That must have been terrifying", is a strong statement. Something like, "Tell me more about it", or "Tell me more" would have allowed him room to share what *it was like for him.*

- At C3: David, another question. Can you see that he answered you? Can you see that questions typically demand an answer? So, you can see how your question, "How did you handle that?" directed the conversation toward an answer. Can you imagine that if you had stated, "Tell me more about it" you would not have got the response, "I prayed". Instead, in all likelihood, he would have begun to share the content of the nightmare.

- At C4: See previous points about asking questions

- At P4: Not really. It didn't last long. I'm sure it was just a dream. Again, you force him to answer you. David, I come from a Policing background, and so asking questions came so naturally to me. In fact, initially I resisted the idea that questions were 'bad' in a pastoral conversation. I thought asking questions demonstrated my interest in the person and their story + it helped me gather more information which would lead to greater understanding. I was wrong! I came to see slowly, that asking questions is a technique used either by beginners who don't know any better or by chaplains who are afraid to enter the 'pit'. David, if you want to avoid a pastoral conversation or in other words, you want to avoid the pit, because the darkness scares you, then keep asking questions!

- At C5: To me, this was a rushed offering of a prayer because you didn't know where to go to. In practice, for a patient that has mentioned God or prayer, I may ask, at the right time, "Would you like me to say a prayer before I leave?" This question, asked at the conclusion of a pastoral conversation, gives choice to the patient. Your question sounds more like a command, even if that is not your intention.

Pastoral Verbatim Report- example student verbatim #4

Name of trainee: Matthew

Date: 3rd January, 2020.

Patients Name: Alice

Denomination: Christian

Marital status: Married

Date written: 3rd January, 2020.

Number of previous visits: Nil

Duration of visit: 20 minutes

Background:

It was my first visit to Alice. She was in the Palliative Care ward, and when I saw her, she appeared tired and drawn. As I entered the room Alice smiled and beckoned me in.

Aim:

To provide a space where Alice could feel she was listened too and valued.

The Groan:

C1: Good morning, Alice. I'm one of the chaplains. How are things with you this morning?

P1: I don't know. I'm taking each day as it comes.

C2: How long have you been here- I don't think you were here last fortnight that I visited?

P2: I was at home, and I took a turn for the worst last Wednesday, unbearable pain. They got me into the hospital quickly, then said they were going to transfer me to another hospital.

C3: You've got a lovely space here, probably got one of the best rooms here.

P3: And one of the best things is my husband Ian took me out in a wheelchair onto the patio and into the sun.

C4: That was a treat. So, your husband is close enough to come visit?

P4: He's been through cancer too. He's a bit wonky on his feet but he's ok. He's been looking after me beautifully and my daughter visits every day. And I can have my family visit, with lounge chairs and TV and the outside patio. And they can even stay overnight in the next room.

C5: Having that option sounds like a real comfort for you.

P5: It just wasn't like being in hospital, all of this is fantastic. When I walked in it didn't look anything like a hospital room. I get a lot of visitors and a lot of friends come. And my husband comes down. He was looking at another hospital, but he couldn't find any beds available in there. But this is a lovely place and if I can't go home this is a lovely place to be.

C6: Are you hoping that you might be able to go home?

P6: No.

C7: So, that's not an option?

P7: No, no. That's what they've said in blunt terms and I'm getting weaker every day. I haven't been able to eat anything for the last four days and my bowels haven't been working. And everything I put into myself just comes back out, so you know that's what's happening.

C8: The cancer really takes a toll.

P8: Yes, cancer and then a hysterectomy and…and thought they had got it all…but cancer returned six months later. Had a bowel obstruction there again, and discovered the cancer was going all through my chest.

C9: You've been through the wars. A lot to be hit with.

P9: Yes, this is my tenth time in hospital and it's a bit of a challenge. The cancers are so advanced that they originally gave me to October.

C10: Well, you have outlasted that one.

(she laughs)

C11: You'll be writing reviews of hospital beds.

P10: Oh yes, you know but this is being the best one. It suits me now.

C12: And you're not too far from your home, so family can visit.

P11: Yes. We built a lovely home in the mountains, and Ian comes frequently to see me, though he's not in good health himself. My daughter got married in the grounds of our home which is beautiful, and we had the reception there because we've got 2.5 acres. But what happened was on that day I started chemo, and my hair fell out on the morning of the wedding.

C13: That must have thrown you?

P12: I said, "I don't need this today", and my daughter took control and she made me a turban.

C14: Sounds like a Maggie Tabberer moment.

P13: And they all thought it was part of the outfit. And I was fine because it came out a few days beforehand and Ian kept me going through that.

C15: He is always your support.

P14: Yeah. I had my pills, and I was dancing on that day.

C16: Terrific that you had such a good day.

P15: I'm just so over the top happy about it and the man she married. I think they were born for each other. It was wonderful. And he came to Ian and me to ask our blessing; they were a couple made for each other.

C17: That's a nice thought; indicates something to you about this person coming into your family. Also, sounds like all these things were a blessing for you amongst everything you were going through.

P16: Exactly. And my daughter was so lovely obviously marrying this man that she adored.

C18: Seems to have been a wonderful occasion and a comfort to you that you were well enough to be present. And obviously a happy day for your daughter.

P17: Such a wonderful young man. He visits me here by himself to check on me and we have lovely chats.

C19: Sounds like he knows he has a great mother-in-law.

P18: And you are a chaplain?

C20: Yes, but not a member of the clergy, but available to offer pastoral care, a chat with patients, or whatever suits them.

P19: I'm interested in talking about what I should be feeling at this stage, the stage at the end? What should I be thinking and feeling, I don't know?

C21: Ok

P20: What do you think I should be feeling, something particular? I'm not sure if I need to know how I should be feeling?

C22: Do you think you should be feeling something in particular?

P21: I don't know if I should be feeling something in particular?

C23: What a question! It's different for every one and I have not had your direct experience. So, you're in a unique position- you're at that point where you're obviously thinking about this. Only you can know your feelings.

P22: I've never been religious. I went to Sunday School. I was in the fellowship church at St. John's church in Sydney. I will never be particularly religious so I wonder what I should be doing and thinking at this great stage in my life?

C24: It's your unique journey. There are things you know-like what's happening now to you- and there are things you feel about that. But I get the sense that you are working through some of those feelings, and hopefully that will lead to a sense of peace in yourself.

P23: I travelled a lot, 36 times overseas, so I have many beautiful memories of that. I have the one child here, took 14 years before that could happen, and my husband and I just had our 50th wedding anniversary. Marriage to a wonderful man. I just want to spend this time with Ian and enjoy what life has given us.

C25: It sounds as though you have had a satisfying and fulfilling life- your travels, in the things you have done with Ian, in the joy you expressed about your daughter and son-in-law.

P24: Yes.

C26: What do you feel you want to do for the time you have left?

P25: I just want quality time with Ian.

C27: Alice, when you asked before what you should be thinking, well I'm hearing about your life and its blessings and family- that's what you are remembering and thinking about. Hopefully, that gives you contentment.

P26: There was talk about taking me home and having a hospital bed there, but I didn't want that because Ian is the only one at home, and I didn't want him getting exhausted. I don't want that to be the last thing he remembers about me. Anyway, after we had a family chat, we all agreed that I should stay here. I do love our house, it reminds me of my travels overseas, but here is better for all of us.

C28: The house seems like a great memento of your travels and life together.

P27: When I had to leave the house for the last time, the ambulance officers were very kind and let me take one last look.

C29: Someone who understood you and wanted to ease the pain of the move.

P28: I just loved that house. It was based on villas we saw in Italy.

C30: And that memory of your house, this last picture you have, and the paramedic talking with you-you want to keep that good memory.

P29: I might have physically left my home, but it is still in my mind.

C31: Seems like it such a strong memory of all your family happy times.

P30: Can I show you photos of the house?

C32: Of course.

P31: It has lovely stone- and here are some with snow a few months ago.

C33: Looks gorgeous.

P32: Some people don't know what's going to happen to them, or they can be scared of the unknown. But they tell me that I will just get weaker and sleepier. I haven't been able to eat anything for a few days, and if I do, it comes out both ends- that's what it is.

C34: Very hard for your body to deal with that.

P33: Some people say they have six months to go, but who can tell? You know some people think or you know that's going to be it. I think you just take it as it is.

C35: It seems you have adjusted your thinking to what you are feeling and are working through that in your own way.

P34: I'll just get more and more exhausted and I'll just go to sleep.

C36: When you said before about what you should be thinking..

P35: I think I believe...I don't know whether I believe in heaven. I don't know if I ever believed in any of those religious things...those doctrines. I believe in God, just having trouble getting my head around all those concepts. I think I believe the spirit goes on. I tell my husband I might be leaving him physically, but I'd always be there in spirit, and I'll never leave him in that way. I believe the spirit is still around and I am fairly attached to the belief that all you do has some effect.

C37: It's your journey, it's unique to you. I sense a strong link you and Ian have. I hope that sustains him. People can tell you I think this happens, or that happens, but it's your journey, it's your experience and hopefully it will be a peaceful and reassuring one for you.

P36: I hope so. Thank you for sitting beside me.

C38: Thank you for sharing your story, Alice.

My response and feedback

At C1 you have not included a choice for them to say, "No thanks" in your introduction. Maybe you did, but I can only comment on what's written. Always give them the opportunity to pass on our offer.

At C2- it's not a bad question early on in the visit, but questions put people on the defensive. It's almost like, "Oh no, I'm being interrogated". I know that sounds exaggerated, and I'm not saying she felt like that, but have a look at the handout I gave you on asking questions. Now, depending how she answered C1, for example, she sounded tired and worn out, you could respond with a statement, for example, "It sounds like you have had enough of this place". Even in early stages of our visit, the avoidance of questions with statements that start with either, (a) It sounds like, or (b) It seems like, can go a long way to that person feeling like this conversation is not like other conversations I have.

At C3- Instead of commenting on the niceties of the hospital, address the sudden urgency of what happened last Wednesday, for example, "It sounds like life went from normal to hellish so quickly". I mean, there are a lot of possible responses, but I'm acknowledging what had happened at home, and giving her room to expand on what she felt etc. last Wednesday. You see, as a result of 'P2' she is talking about being out on the patio, instead of the suddenness and uncertainty of life.

At C4- you are asking questions. Instead, "Tell me more about last Wednesday. That must have been so scary and shocking for you and your husband".

At P4 she mentions her husband has been through cancer etc. She could have just said, "Yes, we live quite close by actually". But she didn't, she brought up something she wants to talk about. You see, when someone brings up something they didn't have to, then guess what- that's the next subject matter to acknowledge. For example, "Wow! So, you both have been through so much already. It must have been scary and stressful going through Ian's treatment for you". Just an example, but it gives her an opportunity to discuss what her husband's cancer meant to her. Instead in P4/P5 she is still talking about the hospital: lounge chairs/TV/patio.

C5: good.

C6: You're not sure what to say, so you ask a question. Even a statement like, "It sounds like you might miss being here when it's time to go home".

C7: A question. Instead, "Oh, tell me more about that" I want to give her an opportunity to tell me more about what, "No" to going home means to her. If I couldn't go home, it would be huge, and for you too I imagine. It's probably of major significance to her as well.

C8: What would it mean to be dying, because that's what happening. So, a statement like, "It sounds like you reached the time of your life when you're running out of time". And then see what she says.

C9 Good- no questions + a statement

C10 ok

C12: Not sure why you brought this up again. Your feeling uncomfortable is all I can guess.

P12- She mentions the husband again. + the chemo and her hair falling out on the wedding day----HUGE

C13 Think of two or three responses to P12

C15 OK

C17 good

C21- Better than a question, but a statement like, "Tell me more about what you're feeling" would encourage her to open up about exactly what her feelings are, and to a lesser extent what are her thoughts about what she is going through.

C22- A question. Instead, "I would love to hear more about what you are feeling".

P22- Only the dead feel nothing….in their body left behind that is. Of course, she is feeling something. Like many older persons, feelings may be something they have shut down for years for many reasons, so helping her to explore those long-avoided feelings would be beneficial…if she chooses too.

C23- Again, avoid questions and make statements. Like the above, "Tell me more about…"

C23- & C24- too long a response. Short statements.

C25- Good, although to 'assist' her with her exploration of where she is at now, something like, "It sounds like you have had a satisfying and fulfilling life, maybe something you are finding it painful to think about that life ending"

C26- Another question, and one she answered in P23.

C27- not sure what the point is with this statement, but at least there was no question.

P32- I think this was Alice's way of bringing up again her uncertainties about what happens after death. I think she is telling you she is scared of the unknown. She knows she is dying, and your response that, "Very hard for your body to deal with" just misses her ultimate concern she is expressing.

P33- Alice gives you one another opportunity to talk about her uncertainties, but again it is missed, with "it seems you are working through it in your own way".

P36- Alice interrupts you to lay out her theology, and you give her the same response as you did in C23 & C24. Then she gave up and said, "Goodbye".

Summary:

I can sense a fair bit of anxiety from you in this verbatim. One indicator of anxiety in a conversation like this is the number of questions. After reading this verbatim I was certain of two things very strongly:

(1) This woman was desperate to speak about her concerns for her husband and (2) her uncertainties about what comes after death, and she didn't really get a chance to. In C4 you asked about how far her husband has to travel to visit (who cares) but she answers: "He's been through cancer too". Matthew, when people tell you something very meaningful (she hadn't mentioned that yet) that you haven't even asked, then they are telling you *what they want to talk about*. Makes it really easy to know, as the chaplain, about one of her ultimate concerns. But you didn't pick up on it. So, in P11, she says again, "Though he's (Ian) not in good health himself", but you missed again.

My advice to you is to relax. People don't know what they don't know. They don't know how good a pastoral conversation can be, and how different it can be from what others are doing. A volunteer said to me, "It's hard to practice when I only come to the hospital 2 hours/week". My response, "Practice every conversation every day". In either a social or pastoral conversation, I notice I do very little different. The more skilled I became the more naturally I stopped asking too many questions even in a social conversation. I continue to practice making statements rather than questions. Try making statements and stop asking questions. Just see how much you can learn from someone without asking a question. It may surprise you.

Whether I'm dealing with my neighbour, a patient in mental health, or a patient dying, what I do stays the same: I create a space where I'm relaxed, listening with attention and intention, trying to understand what is being said directly, or the message behind the message, and feedback responses in the form of a statement that conveys I understand or am striving too. That's it. I know that seems like a lot, but when we started driving it seemed like a lot to remember, but over time it became more unconscious and easier. All the people we visit will have all the questions/advice/silver linings/shared experiences/ and every other unnecessary thing said to them by everyone they know. We strive to be different. Practise every day and in every conversation.

Explore your own inner triggers/fears/concerns/hurts/wounds/ let downs/disappointments/ etc. It's all waiting to be explored within us. This role is more about us than the Other. As you know, we don't drag a person down into their pit, we wait to be invited, but this patient was desperately wanting to drag you down into her pit, but she couldn't get you there. The reasoning's for that only you will discover, but we need to be ready, willing and able to get into the pit whenever we are visiting. Unfortunately, most of the techniques we use to avoid the pit, we are unconscious of, but the evidence is plain to see. So, just assume there is unresolved grief in you, and start to explore and process them, or else you will avoid the pit for your whole ministry.

As you said to me, this verbatim has a lot of learning within it, and you're right. So, lets learn from it. I would love you to pretend to have this encounter over again and make up responses from both you and her based upon your new responses. I also appreciate the length of this verbatim, you remembered a lot. Well done.

<u>Pastoral Verbatim Report- example student verbatim #5</u>

This verbatim is from a student who ministers in a prison.

Name of student: Josh

Date: 3rd January, 2021.

Prisoner's Name: Greg

Denomination: Unknown

Marital status: Divorced

Date written: 3rd January, 2021.

Number of previous visits: 3

Duration of visit: 20 minutes

Aim: To be a listening ear to Greg and assist him to regain his focus.

<u>The Groan:</u>

C1: Hi Greg. Good that we have a chance to meet up again today.

G1: Chaplain I have some bad news. My lawyer tells me my sentence could be between eight and ten years.

C2: How awful. Your emotions must be all over the place. How is your body feeling?

G2: It's as if I'm falling down a long way and when I hit bottom the sentence begins. It's as if I'm possessed by demons.

C3: Demons? That must be scary. I know I would be.

G3: Yes, it is. No one believed it was me who was on the news that night. I was angry that it happened. I know that God sees everything. I'm no good at anything. I never have been. I pray every day, but it doesn't help.

C4: Greg, just by listening to you I can hear the good in you. You're feeling angry, ashamed and depressed. I believe you're a good person. It's you who doesn't believe it. Remember, God always loves you as His love never changes despite our actions.

G4: My lawyer told me I was too honest with the Police. I told them everything and they gave me this violent charge. I'm not violent. Now I'm sleeping with demons. It's like a steam train hitting you and I've been hit hard. I'm possessed.

C5: Greg, we have met about three times and you're not describing the person I know. The person you're telling me about sounds like someone else. You are definitely not possessed.

G5: Yes, it's me. I'm beside myself. The physiologist saw me and it was just something he had to do. He took notes and didn't really care. He walked out and went and saw someone else. Then he goes home and forgets about it. You're different. You listen.

C6: Thank you. We are all different. It's not so much that I listen. I can see the goodness in you. Scripture tells us that we are a reflection of God. There are elements in our DNA that somehow reflects God's love and I sense it in you. It's strong. You're a good man with a good heart.

G6: I think I know that, but it doesn't help just knowing. I want to be a better person. My sister is suffering, my nephew keeps asking for me. If my mum dies while I'm here, I don't know what I'll do.

C7: Sounds scary. Yes, I would be feeling depressed as well. I don't normally ask people why they are feeling so bad about themselves, but you have me mystified. What went wrong?

G7: I got onto ICE. I felt empty. I didn't want to socialise. I smoked that stupid shit. My heart hurts. Even had some yesterday. Got it from one of the guys. I know it's an escape. Don't feel good today because I took that shit.

C8: I hear the desperation. Yet you are a care giver for your mum, and a role model for your nephew, and yet you escape by using drugs. What are you escaping from?

G8: I just needed more. I was gambling online. Spent $40,000 in one night and needed more money. I went to the pub, pointed a gun at their head and demanded money.

C9: Wow! Greg, thank you for sharing the incident. You didn't have too. It sounds like an addiction.

G9: I want to do a drug rehab course but no one here talks to me about that. It's only a matter of time before that grenade goes off. I've always been a failure.

C10: You're not a failure. You just haven't found the right answers. It's good to hear you talk about a drug rehab program. Keep asking that question to whoever you see. You are not trapped by your past. You have the potential to reform and get better. You are the creator of your future.

G10: Yeah, ok, but that's not helping me now. I feel possessed.

C11: I understand what you are saying and it must feel like being in the pit of despair. Keep focused on the here and now. This is where you begin to pick yourself up, that is, if you really want to. You are a brave person to be thinking of rehab. You're not a failure, it's just a false start. I believe in your ability to be a better yourself.

G11: Chaplain, can you come back to see me?

C12: Of course, I will.

<u>My Feedback</u>

Thanks for this verbatim, Josh. As I read through your verbatim, I could sense that you were not really listening and empathising, but rather you were trying to fix how Greg saw himself. Following are some pointers:

C1: I assume that this meeting between the two of you was arranged, as no choice was offered to Greg to refuse the offer of a visit.

C2: Not sure where, "How is your body feeling?" this statement comes from. I can only imagine it comes from an agenda you have. Stick with feeding back emotions and loss statements about his "bad news".

C3: Not bad. You don't need to add, "I know I would be". Simply acknowledging how scary it would feel to feel that you are "possessed by demons" is enough.

C4: This is your first attempt to 'fix' how Greg sees himself. Greg does go on to tell you clearly that this approach "does not help", but you don't listen. If someone says, "I'm no good at anything, I never have been", then it is not helpful to argue with how they feel. We need to feedback that we are both listening and understanding, for example, "It sounds like failure is something you're used to" or "It sounds like you feel like a waste of space". This is not being harsh, but simple echoing what Greg feels. He can either say, "Yes, exactly", or he could say, "Well, I'm not a complete waste of space, as I am a role model for my nephew and I do care for my mum". However, offering a fix helps no one.

C5: You're not listening, even though Greg tells you in G5 that you listen, you're not listening. You are arguing with how Greg sees himself in an attempt to make him feel better, but in G6 he tells you clearly, "It doesn't help just knowing", and in G10 he says, "But that's not helping me now". One of many different responses to G4 could be, "It feels like there is someone else in control of you, and you have little to no control in your own life". Again, this leaves room for Greg to 'supervise' how close he believes our response came to his reality.

C6: Fix. You are yelling at the top of Greg's 'pit', but you have not joined him in the 'pit'. A possible response to G5 could have been, 'It sounds like you were just a task for him to complete before he left for the day", or, "It seemed like you were so unimportant to him, almost invisible". Anything like that is better than offering a fix in an attempt for you to feel better, for you to feel like you have helped someone. You have forgotten how it is we do help, and as a result, you are actually unhelpful in your responses.

C7: You started well with, "Sounds scary", and it should have ended with that. What followed was your curiosity. "What went wrong" is irrelevant to the here and now. Anyone in prison has a story about what went wrong but explaining that to the chaplain is nothing other than your failure to contain your curiosity.

C8: Another useless question: "Escape from what". It doesn't matter at all. Anyone who is smoking ICE is escaping hurt/pain/disappointment/trauma etc. The specific trauma is unimportant when I'm in the 'pit'. Respond to the emotions or the losses and contain the curiosity.

C10: You're arguing again with him and offering advice and solutions. Even though Greg tells you that you are not helping him, in C11 you are offering him more advice and trying hard to get Greg to see himself as you do, which is not our task.

Josh, it seems like you lost your way in this encounter. There was a tension I felt reading this verbatim, because you were desperate to help Greg reframe how he saw himself. Even Greg reminded you that this was unhelpful. When we argue with someone about how they see themselves, then that person is going to feel misunderstood and angry. Who is a better judge of ourselves than ourselves? So, if I say to someone, "I feel like a fat ugly pig" and they say, "No, you are beautiful and made in the image and likeness of God", that is just BS to me, so don't waste your breath lying to me. It's annoying that you need to lie to me to somehow try and make me feel better about myself! What I want is understanding, for example, "It sounds like you hate who you are right now", or "It sounds like you wish you were someone else".

In your 'Aim' you state, "…assist him regain his focus", this is the problem. You want to help him regain his focus, how he sees things, and Greg just wants you to understand where he is at. Greg is in a very deep and dark 'pit' and you were unwilling to 'jump' in, and the reason for that is for you to find, but it is imperative that you discover the reason you didn't want to enter his darkness.

Pastoral Verbatim Report- example student verbatim #5

Name of student: Lynn
Date: 14th December, 2020.
Patient's Name: Susan
Denomination: Unknown
Marital status: Widow
Date written: 14th December, 2020.
Number of previous visits: 0
Duration of visit: 20 minutes

Background:

Visited Patient in hospital while doing ward rounds. She was keen to share about her husband who died a month ago and what their life has been like for the past 70 years of marriage.

<u>Aim:</u>

Giving the patient an opportunity to share whatever they wanted to share.

<u>The Groan:</u>

C1- Good morning. My name is Lynn and I am a chaplain here at Nepean Hospital. Would you like to have a chat?

P1-Yes, I would thank-you. I am feeling a bit sad right now and would like to talk about it if you have the time.

I asked to sit and we started to chat!

C2- What is causing you to be sad?

P2- My husband died a month ago and I was just looking at his picture here *(she picked up their wedding photo and gave it to me to look at)* and remembering the good times.

C3 – Good times

P3-We had been married for 70 years and have lived in Sydney for 60 years. We raised our 5 children and now we have 7 wonderful grandchildren.

C4- 70 years Married that's amazing

P4- You know it seems like it was yesterday. We had our difficulties like everyone else but we never were angry at each other for long. We would both start talking to each other about 5-10 minutes after we supposed to be not talking to each other!

I laughed

C5 – What a lovely Wedding dress in the picture, is that satin?

P5- My girlfriend at the time knew what I wanted for my wedding day and made it for me as a gift.

C6-How special

P6- I remember that it was such a lovely day and a beginning for being together and happy ever since.

We sat quiet for a couple of minutes

P7- What church do you belong to.

C7: My husband and I attend …... Do you attend anywhere local?

P8- I went to the Anglican church at Cambridge Park until recently. I had a disagreement with the minister when he said that it was my fault that my husband did not attend church. My husband was the most beautiful and generous person I have ever know and I got so hurt that he thought bad of my husband so I stopped going.

C9:- so hurtful

P9-I have spoken to my family, and they agree that I was right in leaving but I do miss going to church.

C10-I can see that it would be hard for you

We spoke a bit more about her family and even thought she was close to them all she did not know how she was going to manage without her husband. Not sure how she was going to cope with being alone

I found it difficult not to get too emotional speaking with her, as she shared her marriage with such love for her husband and the grief was so fresh.

I am aware after speaking with Neil and Michael that I need to be careful not to ask questions and phrase my response differently.

Lynn.

My Feedback

C1- Good intro with clear choice.

C2-ok. Remember, think about statements rather than questions. For example, "Tell me about the sadness"

C3: ok, but I would have offered more than just repeating what she had just said, for example, even just nodding smiling and making the "Mmmmm" sound.

C4 ok

C5: to me this is an indication of you being uncomfortable. Responding to the loss of a husband and all that means, is more important than the material of the wedding dress. Often, when we don't know what to say and so we are tempted to ask a question. Try not to ask any questions in a pastoral conversation. In P4 she says something meaningful, and a thoughtful response to let her know you are listening and understanding or trying to understand what this significant loss means to her. For example, "It sounds like there was such a wonderful bond between you both. Life will never be the same again for you and your family". There are a thousand different responses, so try and imagine what it would be like to lose a husband of so many years, and feed that back.

Also, the question about the wedding dress is like all questions: they demand an answer. So, instead of this woman being in the space of remembering her husband and the good times they had, and sharing that with you, the question took her away from that to explaining about the dress in P5.

P6 needed some response, and when no response came, she asked a question about you. That usually signal the end of the pastoral question, or at least heading toward the end.

C7: you answer her question and then ask another question. This question as well leads the conversation in another direction.

C9: This is better than a question, but is really just parroting her. Think of another response to P8. There are again a thousand responses to convey some level of understanding, for example, "It sounds like he thought poorly of you as well, and that you were angry enough to not go back anymore". Now, she may say, "Oh I wasn't angry, I was disappointed". It doesn't matter if I 'miss' what was going on for her, as long as she senses that I'm with her and trying to understand. Again, another possible response, "So painful to lose your worshipping community and all that support". She may say, "Oh no, I still have all my friends from the Church, and I have made new friends in my new church". It doesn't matter. Remember the training: listen for a loss or an emotion. Hear a loss, ask yourself **what is the emotion behind the loss** (sadness, anger, frustration, fear, bitterness, etc) and feed the emotion back. Hear an emotion, ask yourself **what is the loss behind the emotion**, as in the above case: the loss of understanding from her minister; the loss of the Church community; the loss of justice, as she is blamed for her husband's behaviour; the loss of compassion and love from the minister etc) and feed that back.

C10: find another word instead of 'hard'. Imagine if you had to leave your church because the minister (person representing God) misunderstood you and judged incorrectly about a situation, such that you had to leave, for example, bitter disappointment; gutted; betrayed; abandoned; furious; lost; broken-hearted; devastated; etc.

I know that it's not easy to change patterns of communication that we have used and practiced everyday of our lives up to now. It takes a conscious effort to contain our solutions/advice/curiosities/ questions/ shared experiences etc. Practice in EVERY conversation, not just here but with everyone. Every conversation, treat like it's a pastoral conversation. Keep reflecting on your practice and emotional triggers.

Chapter Eleven

Managing Triggers

Imagine you're driving in your car, and you notice the engine light on your dashboard come on. What do you do? Most people would take their car in to get serviced, to find out why the engine light came on and to fix the issue, so it doesn't light up any more. The service department would determine why the light is coming on and fix whatever the issue is. Soon, you're back on the road, driving again. Being aware of your emotions is like being aware of your engine light. When you notice an emotion come up, take note and ask yourself why is this emotion surfacing? Emotions you may notice: anger, sadness, frustration, jealousy, fear, doubt, and even resistance.

Not all emotional triggers are the same. Emotional triggers are stimuli that can at times provoke an automatic, intense emotional reaction within us. Triggers can include people, words, memories, smells, sounds, intrusive thoughts, opinions, behaviours or other specific personal situations. Emotional triggers can set off a wide range of feelings, but remember, triggers explain, they don't excuse our behaviour. On the one hand, triggers may engender feelings of anger, sadness, anxiety, guilt, shame, fear or panic. People may experience these feelings in their bodies, often characterized by headaches or feeling a knot in their throat or butterflies in their stomach. Others externalize their emotions by, for example, arguing with a co-worker or a family member or cutting off a driver, road rage. In fact, some are positive and make us feel happy or proud. I knew a patient who shared with me that she lived alone and often felt lonely and sad. In order to help herself, she would take out family photo albums. She could easily spend hours looking at pictures and reminiscing. These visual memories would always make her feel happy and less lonely.

Ewan Kelly (2012) writes of the importance and courage required by chaplains to have examined their own inner world and emotional triggers in order to be even able to step into someone else's darkness:

Unless we are aware, to some degree, of what and who we are, how much of the other are we really going to see, hear, feel or understand? Moreover, not only do we need to be cognizant of our own inner landscape, we need to be reasonably comfortable with it as we seek to create a safe space with, and for, patients and parishioners to be themselves. The Dutch pastor and spiritual guide Henri Nouwen reflects: What does hospitability as healing power require? It requires first of all that *the host feel at home in his own house,* and secondly, that he create a *free and fearless place for the unexpected visitor.* (1979, 89).

I clearly remember my interview for the position of chaplain at Nepean Hospital. One of the essential aspects of the role covered was the reminder of the importance of professional supervision. I remember replying that I was well aware of the clear need for this aspect of my role and assured all present of my intent to organise such supervision. In my head of course, I said, "With what I saw and experienced in the Police Force, there was nothing I would encounter as a chaplain that would 'rattle my cage'. I had no intention of wasting my time discussing 'upsetting' things. I couldn't have been more wrong.

It was a Friday afternoon, and I was looking forward to getting an early start to the weekend. I had packed my stuff ready to leave early, when a pager tone alerted me to a call from a patient. I was not enthusiastic! I took down the details hurriedly and walked with a purpose toward the ward and room in question. I was thinking, "Why does this woman wait until 4.30pm on a Friday to ask for a chaplain?" I got to the room and walked straight in, only to be met by a man in his thirties. I said, "Oh, excuse me. I am one of the hospital chaplains, and I think I have made a mistake and come to the wrong room". What follows is a verbatim of the conversation that took place between us. 'P' is patient, and 'C' chaplain.

P1: Oh, that's ok. I am getting discharged shortly. Are you a Catholic?

C2: Yes, I am.

P2: Um…I was born a Catholic, but some terrible things happened to me and my brother by Catholic priests & sisters, and now I just can't go in a Catholic Church. I mean, I have been thinking lately, the last couple of years, that I would like to go back into a Catholic Church. I like the statues, incense, and stuff like that, but when I have tried, I just can't bring myself to enter.

C3: It seems like whatever happened is still powerful enough to stop you at the Church door.

P3: When I was 8 years old, my parents sold me and my twin brother into a paedophile ring. I know that sounds unbelievable, and I wish it was. We were sold to a man that worked with St John's ambulance. But he wasn't the worst one. There were others, older, higher up. Police, judges, doctors, and priests. We would both be handed around these 2 or 3 groups. But we stayed with the man from the ambulance. He lived with his parents. His mum would wash and clean our school clothes, but we were not allowed to speak to her. She never spoke with us, never looked at us. His father would come home, and get drunk and go to bed, and then when both his parents were in bed, he would come in and...well you can guess (starts to cry).

C4: How absolutely horrific. You must have felt so betrayed by your parents

P4: (Nodding) My brother committed suicide a few years ago now...He was the strong one physically, and I was the thinker...he just couldn't handle the memories and nightmares anymore. Most of the time the groups would abuse us one at a time, and sometimes to protect him, I would pretend to be him when they had finished with me, and I would go and take more...just to protect him...but in the end he killed himself...

C5: You loved him so much that you were willing to take such terrible abuse in his place

P5: Yes, I did love him. I wanted to go back and knock on the door of the man who did this to us and kill him with an iron bar...but I am still scared of him, even though he must be in his seventies now, if not dead! When we were twelve we ran away, and when they (Police) caught us, my mum and step-dad couldn't be found, so they sent us to South Australia to a Catholic boarding school. Gee Michael…they treated us worse than dogs. (Crying)

C6: You must have felt so desperately alone and hopeless.

P6: We did… The nuns… they were so cruel. I remember once that one of them had a long ruler, longer than your arm, and she hit me so hard across the back that I wet my pants. Well, did I get it then. She pulled me into a classroom, and she made me take all my clothes off, while she called me names…you know, "baby", "moron", "Cry baby" and then she made my brother take me to the shower and wash me. After the shower, she made my brother and I walk on the grass without shoes because there were so many sharp, large thorned bindies. After we did that for a while, she called us in and thrashed us both with an ironing cord. My brother had done nothing, but he got it as bad as me. I always remember that he copped it because of me that day.

C7: Such a terribly sad situation to be in. People who were supposed to represent God, and all they did was hurt and mistreat you.

P7: At the time, we just wanted to be there for each other. At the same time, it made it hard to see him suffer, and strangely, it might have been easier if I was all alone. But he left me in the end. I wondered myself about following him, I couldn't see any hope in my life when he killed himself. (Crying)

C8: How terribly dark and lonely it must have been for you at that time

P8: Terrible, really terrible time for me. Now, I don't have any other family. I wouldn't even know if my parents were alive or dead, not that I really care, but I do wonder now and then. I have so many questions for my mum. I don't understand why she gave us up. Drugs I guess, but I don't know for sure. Do you get it? I have to somehow make sense of it.

C9: You need to know how a mother can be so heartless, and abandon her boys to monsters

P9: That's a good way to describe them; you're right, they were monsters. **(Nurse comes in to Discharge Ray).** Oh, Michael, sorry to dump all that on you. I am not even sure why I did, but thank you for listening, it helps. I didn't want to ruin your day.

C8: Ray, I want you to know that I feel privileged that you shared your story with me. You are very courageous in doing so, and I am grateful that we had this time together before you left the hospital.

P8: Thanks again, Michael.

I had only been in my role about 2 months when this 'mistake' with Ray occurred. I was aware as I struggled to listen to him, that very powerful emotions were rising within me. I so badly wanted to just run to the nearest toilet and cry my eyes out for these poor little boys who had suffered from the hands of so many monsters. In truth, I was happy to be interrupted by the nurse. I returned to my office, and I cried and reflected for some time over their terrible and unnecessary suffering. I called my wife and told her I would be late. I wrote up that conversation which had been seared into my short-term memory. I realised three things that evening as I stayed and processed my feelings and thoughts till nearly 9pm: (1) God doesn't make mistakes. I was meant to meet Ray that afternoon; (2) Verbatims are a powerful way for me to purge what I was feeling, and they would become such a valuable tool in the improving of my practice; and (3) I needed professional supervision. I never wanted to feel like that again, and so I decided the following Monday morning to start my search for a supervisor. However, God took care of this for me, because 0930 Monday morning, a lady contacted the Pastoral Care Department and said, "Hello, my name is Pam. I professionally supervise chaplains and I have just today started a practice near the hospital, and thought I would call and introduce myself". Shortly after this providential call, I began to see Pam monthly. I remember telling her about this encounter with Ray, and how "I never wanted to feel like that again". Pam said, "I would be more worried if you didn't feel the way you did hearing such a horrific story, and I will help with some strategies to make this less impactful on you as you go about your ministry in the hospital".

I wanted to share some of those strategies that have assisted me with my triggers, and a brief outline of how triggers interfere with the work that we undertake here in the hospital.

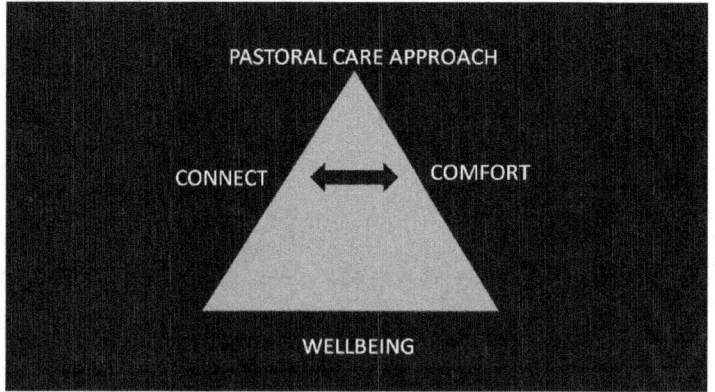

The first area which has a profound impact on my overall ability to perform this ministry is 'wellbeing'. You can see in the above image that at it's very basic level, in connecting with another comfort is transferred. However, that simple statement hangs on my wellbeing. I will not spend any more time mentioning the importance of self-care in this role, a role that so many end up suffering from compassion fatigue and the like. We are a multi-faceted creature and we need to be balancing our whole self in such a way that we ensure longevity in this ministry.

So, what are emotional triggers? Since I have no formal qualifications in psychology or the like, I will state in a simple manner, that a trigger is *an experience that draws us back into the past and causes old feelings and behaviours to arise.* These emotions therefore generally relate to specific experiences from our past history. It will usually involve an external stimulus, such as a smell, or a sound (like a song), or will arise when one of our cherished beliefs are challenged or threatened. These emotional triggers can be of varying intensity, but they generally interfere in our task in a number of ways:

➢ <u>The chaplain will engage in self talk</u>- for example with Ray in the above verbatim, I was scolding these 'God' people for their treatment of Ray and his brother. I was thinking about my twin brother, Mark, and what would it have been like for Mark and I to have gone through this experience.

➢ The chaplain will be tempted to end the interaction prematurely. For me, one of the main reasons for seeking assistance with my triggers was so I wouldn't be tempted to 'run' from such a tragic story. I do want to make the point however, that there may come a time, when in spite of what you would like, ending such a interaction can be the most ideal thing to do. If I simply cannot listen anymore to a terrible story of woe, then it is wrong to pretend to be listening. It would be better to say something like, "I want to say that the story you are sharing is so powerful, and I must say that right now, I am feeling too overwhelmed to continue. Would it be ok if I asked another chaplain to visit and continue with them"? I get this is not ideal, but again, if the listening has stopped, then it's better to be honest with the person.

- ➢ The chaplain is emotionally overwhelmed. In the above verbatim this was certainly the case for me.
- ➢ The chaplain may be hesitant to engage further with others. I know this is how I initially felt following the above verbatim. I sat thinking to myself, "I don't need to go through that again, but how do I avoid feeling like that in this role?" If one doesn't take the active steps required to mitigate the effect of emotional triggers on ourselves, then going and doing something else for a living becomes very attractive.

➢ The Chaplain may avoid taking a person deeper in the future. Okay, so you don't want to give up your ministry as a chaplain, but you consciously or perhaps unconsciously engage with the Other in such a manner that an 'invitation' to enter their 'pit' never comes. It is really quite easy to avoid the 'pit' should that be your intention. We are all well-versed in this behaviour, because it typically consists in doing everything possible to maintain the elements of a social conversation. The Other will pick up on this and receive the message: "This is the depth I'm comfortable with, thanks".

➢ We may avoid the type of patients that are more likely to trigger us, for example, I may avoid going to see any Oncology patients, or Dementia patients, because these trigger painful memories of loved ones who suffered from these conditions.

These are just some of the ways that our untouched emotional triggers can interfere with our task of joining the Other in the darkness.

So, you know you have these triggers: how do we as chaplains manage them in such a way that they become a strength? Like most things, it begins with awareness of their existence. In my experience, awareness of triggers is fairly obvious due to their power. You are engaging with another, and because of what is being shared, you become aware of a shift in your body and/or emotions. Of course, awareness is not enough. I'm constantly telling my chaplains and volunteers: "Reflect on your practice. Why did you say so and so? What happened for the Other when you did that? How did what you say change the direction of the conversation (if it did)? Reflect on your practice. Be mindful of what's happening for you, and ask why is this happening? What needs or set of needs are you responding to?"

So, in line with triggers, ask yourself, "Things were going really well, and then they mentioned being betrayed by a family member, and I suddenly had knots in my stomach, and I felt irate". In this instance you figure out two things: (1) awareness of a shift, and (2) what the *external* stimuli was in all probability, in this case: betrayal. Here is where the temptation to stop working enters. Here is the point where one needs courage, because here is where I need to go back in my history and locate this oft forgotten event which has just been fired off. This is the exercise in hindsight: locate the *internal* stimuli. I was constantly surprised just how easy it was to remember forgotten incidents, mainly from my childhood, which became readily accessible with some reflective meditation on my past. Time and time again I would remember things I hadn't thought about in more than 50 years. I did make consistent effort in this regard, especially in the first two years of this role, because I was being triggered fairly regularly to some degree, and I owed it to the Other to be in a state that I could work effectively as a chaplain. Ewan Kelly puts it this way:

The greatest asset which any of us offers to another in caring relationships is ourselves, or to be more precise, our reflexive selves- the self which we have reflected on. Such awareness does not happen easily nor without intention or experience to reflect on and time in which to do so. Such ongoing reflexivity can be arduous and painful at times, as well as creative and rewarding. It is the stuff of formation and reformation, shaping not just who we are but, more importantly, who we perceive we are. (p.5)

At this point, using both my supervisor and researching the topic, I developed a number of strategies which has helped me reduce the strength and power of my triggers. I have not removed any of my triggers but have reduced their impact to the degree they do not interfere with my ability to engage in a pastoral conversation, and be willing to enter the darkness of another.

Strategy (1) <u>Use of the Family Genogram Tool</u>

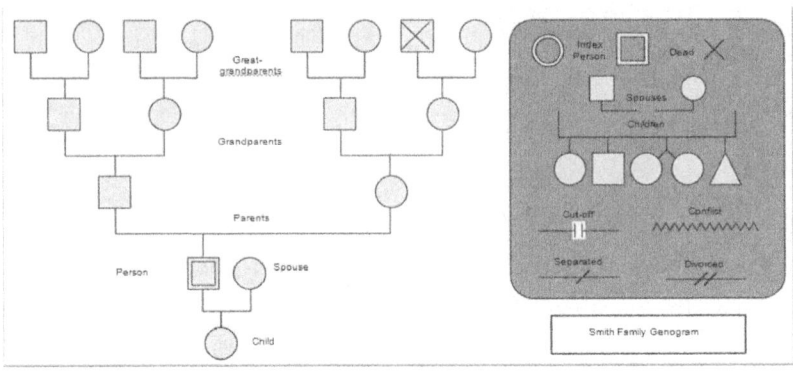

My supervisor suggested that I fill out my own Family Genogram, as a means to understand *generationally* the source of some of my triggers. For example, if a chaplain is triggered when a person is expressing anger, it may be that anger was something their family really struggled with. It may remind them of being a child with an angry, drunk and violent father, and as a result, want little to do with a person who starts becoming angry about their situation, or the problems within our Health system. They will attempt to calm the person, rationalise with them, do all they can to feel in control at that time. I had a minor trigger even with this suggestion from my supervisor, because as she outlined what was involved, I became aware of how dysfunctional my family tree was, and I didn't like to think that she was going to see it all laid out in front of her. I always tried to project a certain amount of stability and normality, but this would be permanently stained once she got a look at my Family Genogram. Whilst I felt uncomfortable sharing my completed Genogram with my supervisor, she pointed out that whilst "not perfect" I had the ability going forward to have a very conscious and deliberate impact of what would be 'passed down'

from this point. I know that's a sort of fix, but it filled me with hope, and that was what I needed right then and there.

Strategy (2) <u>The use of Verbatim's/and Journaling</u>

I had quickly come to see the value of the verbatim tool. It not only served to act as a means of 'cleaning' myself from what I had heard in an interaction, but I soon realised how valuable a learning tool it was. In regards to my triggers, I could write up a verbatim very methodically, and then at my leisure, investigate, prod and probe all the richness that was contained within it. I could reflect on my part in the interaction; I could quickly see what exactly was the source 'word' or image that had triggered me; I could play around imagining different responses to the person and how that might have affected the interaction.

On average I wrote at least one verbatim a week, so after two years, I had well over 100 verbatims from which I could continue to wring knowledge, and occasionally wisdom from. I could take these verbatims to my supervision sessions, and also give them to my other mentors for constructive criticism.

When training new volunteers, I stress that a requirement for volunteering at the hospital is to provide me a verbatim of a PC at least once per month. It is the only real way to 'keep an eye' on what is being said and done out in the hospital. A verbatim from one of the volunteers allows the learning process to continue for them and the other volunteers, because I change the details and forward the verbatim to them. They have an opportunity to reflect on their thoughts about the verbatim, and to come up with alternative responses. In my turn, I send my feedback to all the volunteers, and so the learning continues for me, as these verbatims force me to reflect on what has been written, and to come up with example responses that will demonstrate to the volunteers what I'm expecting.

A significant benefit of journaling is it is an easy method of self-improvement, as it provides an ongoing opportunity to reflect on a moment in time and therefore it provides a means to get in touch with our emotions and make sense of our feelings. Journaling allows us to see changes over time in our practice, as well as in regards our beliefs and values. I have found journaling an invaluable resource for the management of my emotional triggers, and as an ongoing documented means toward a kind of self-therapy.

The Photo Album

Many years ago, I began a three-year degree in Counselling. What attracted me to this particular course was the combination of theory and practice: each week we would participate in Group Work. On the very first night there was a lady in my group, and I realised straightaway that there was something I didn't like about her. If she made any comment that was vague, or off topic, I would 'be right on to her'. I worked her pretty hard that evening. Before I left the facilitator asked me to remain for a "quick word". He pointed out me that it hadn't gone unnoticed how I treated this fellow student. He told me that other group members had gone off topic and "rambled on" and I didn't address that at all. Hearing this I was uncomfortable. He suggested that I "look through my photo album for any clues". He explained due to my confused look, that it may just be that she reminds me of someone from my past and that it would be worth investigating. What a strange idea I thought. However, I did spend some time that week thinking about whether or not she reminded me of someone. Before the next weeks class I had discovered her near identical copy in my "Photo Album", or affectionately, The Mugshot Book. This lady was very similar to a second-class teacher who I remembered had bullied me, and on a number of occasions had literally punched me in the stomach winding me. Amazing to think back about a teacher behaving like that. I could then plainly see how I had bullied this lady in my class. I resolved to attend the next class with a clear distinction between who this person was before me and my old teacher. I explained to my facilitator, and even spoke with this lady in my class on out Supper Break, and it turned out we became good friends and stay in touch to this day.

I am aware this situation is a projection from me onto another person but following the projection I am triggered into a thoughtless response. There have been quite a few times as I walked toward a particular room on a ward, I have seen the patient and had a similar quick judgement about them, in such a way my instinct was to avoid them. I choose not to avoid, but tell myself that whatever I am feeling as a result of the 'look' of another person, it's not based in reality, and that I should continue in and treat them like anybody else.

Active Imagination

The use of the tool of active imagination made an incredible difference to the strength and power of my emotional triggers. I don't know why such a thing works, but I know it does with me. I want to share an incident from my early school years as an example of how the use of basically 'playing pretend' has assisted me enormously with the issue of triggers.

I was in First class at my local Catholic School, so about 5-6 years old. I remember it was just before the start of school, and that I was running to get to the toilet before our school assembly, which we had each morning. In my haste to get to the toilet, I tripped over and wet my pants. The school principal witnessed this happening as she was coming outside to get ready to commence the assembly. This nun, yelled at me to come to her, and when I reached her, she grabbed me roughly by my shirt collar and told me to come to her office. Once there, she gave me the cane four times on one hand, and then she pulled out a baby's dummy and hung it around my neck. She then took me outside and stood me in front of the assembly and called me "baby" and shared what I had done. She then had a chair brought from inside, and I was told to stand on the chair so everybody could see me, and after assembly she left me on that chair, by myself outside on display, till Little Lunch, two hours later. Looking back I can only imagine how embarrassing and scary that must have been for that little boy.

When I was exploring my strong response to Ray's story above, I uncovered this episode that I had all but forgotten. I decided that somewhere inside of me this little boy was still scared and vulnerable. I know this may sound ridiculous, but for me, I only ask if something works or not: that's the criteria of worth. I imagined going back in time, and seeing this boy standing on this chair from outside the school. I remember looking around the neighbourhood, and recognising how much it had all changed in 50 years. I approached the boy and had the following dialogue:

Me: Hello, what's your name?

Boy: Michael (shyly)

Me: Wow! That's my name too, so it means I will never forget your name (smiling) Climb down off that chair.

Boy: I better not, as I will get into trouble

Me: I promise you won't. C'mon step down. (Boy climbs down) Let me remove this for you (taking off the dummy). That's better. (He nods, looking around sheepishly).

Boy: What if Sister X comes, I will get in trouble again, and so will you.

Me: Sister X is gone now, and there is only you and me. I just had a thought, but first let me ask you a question: Do you have a big brother?

Boy: No, I'm the oldest. I have a twin brother and a smaller brother.

Me: Would you like a BIG BROTHER, someone like me?

Boy: (Nodding and smiling) Do you have a big brother?

Me: No, but I would love to be your big brother. Would you like that?

Boy: Ok, but what would that mean?

Me: Well, you are a big brother to your brothers, so what do you do for them?

Boy: I look after them, and help them with things mum asks, and we play together.

Me: Well, we could do the same. In fact, in my pocket I have something very special. Would you like to see?

Boy: (Eyes wide open and looking toward my pocket as my hand enters)

Me: (Opening my hand, I reveal a beautiful golden whistle). Do you know what this is, Michael?

Boy: (nodding) A little whistle.

Me: Yes, it's little but its magical

Boy: Really? What magic does it have?

Me: Whenever you blow this whistle, I will come. It doesn't matter where I am, or what's happening, when you want me, just blow the whistle and I will hear it and come immediately.

Boy: For true?

Me: Yep. If you want to play, or you feel scared or angry or anything. Just blow the whistle and I will come.

Boy: (Smiling)

Me: I know that there are times we get scared, but most of the time that's because we are alone. But you're not ever going to be alone again. If anything happens that you don't like, you blow your whistle, and your big brother will be here. (I take the string from the dummy and thread the whistle onto it, and place around Michael's neck). So, you see, it's right there when you need it.

Boy: Thank you, Michael.

Me: I know there is an ice cream shop around the corner. Let's go and get one. What's your favourite flavour?

Boy: Double chocolate.

Me: Me too.

There are times that I have been invited into the dark 'pit' of someone, and I can feel 'little Michael' standing beside me hanging on to my leg. He feels safe there, and he waits until I am finished with that person, and then we share what was going on. Over time, his trust in me has grown strong and confident, and as a result, the many powerful and strong emotions that I could be flooded with have greatly reduced. Not disappeared mind you, but reduce. Instead of an '8' or '9' on my Richter scale, it's usually a '1', '2', or '3'. This means that when I am with someone traveling through their dark inner world, I can stay focused on the Other, and be who I need to be for that person to be comforted and transformed.

Benefits for chaplains who face their triggers

- In opening to our own suffering from life losses, we enhance our desire to be of service to those around us. Once I become more comfortable with the 'darkness' within me, the less I worry about the 'darkness' of another.

- We become truly available at deeper levels of our souls. We don't deny pain but open to it and learn what it is trying to teach us. It's understandable, that we may not wish to re-visit horrible times in our life, I know, but the learning and peace that comes from this effort is well worth it. One will never achieve having a non-anxious presence without this effort and work.

- We gain emotional self-awareness. We thereby minimise the power emotional triggers have over us. It is not usual at all for emotional triggers to cause a physical response in us, such as, upset stomach, nausea and vomiting, feeling dizzy, sweating to name a few. A chaplain cannot work experiencing such symptoms, and therefore if the inner work is not done by us, when we will employ other strategies to avoid the 'pits' in others. We simply cannot avoid being triggered as chaplains, or in any other sphere of life.

- We have a greater awareness of when the Other is being emotionally triggered.

- We are aware when we are transferring onto people in the present.

- We can use our emotional triggers to our advantage. We may have so-called 'negative' triggers, but we also have positive triggers, and we can of course, establish new habits which will create new wanted behaviours. The new positive trigger just needs to be specific and actionable immediately. For example, if I want to create a habit in which I'm reading more, then putting a book beside my bed encourages me to read a few pages before sleep.

Remember, our triggers are part of our survival strategy. We link powerful events that scared us or hurt us to those specific stimuli in order to protect us going forward. A person who was struck by lightning may go running at the first rumble of thunder or first rain drop, even though statistically it's unlikely to be struck by lightning twice.

I have often thought that the majority of what it means to be an effective chaplain has to do with myself. Working on the areas that are within me, in order to be really present for another. This requires courage, but we owe it to the patients we visit to have done this work or at least be working on our own inner terrain in order not to utilise all the ways possible to sabotage the encounter we are in. We spend so much of our lives happily avoiding the regrets/hurst/wounds and sufferings of our past, that the older we get the harder this inner work can be. Many chaplains are, shall we say, more mature, and have typically managed to avoid the things in their past they don't want to face, and then they come to chaplaincy and have all these triggers going off, and have a choice to make face them or be ineffective. The choice is yours to make as well. Wuellner (1985, p. 15) states:

How many of us are trying to "wash the feet" of others when we ourselves need help? How fully, freely, and wholly can we reach out to others when we ourselves are inwardly broken and hungry? The first step for transforming this world's pain is to look with honesty   at   our   own   pain.

Chapter Twelve

Managing the "Why God?" Question

Sooner rather than later, a chaplain will hear the "Why God?" question. It typically unfolds along these lines: a patient will state, "All my life I have been a faithful follower of the Lord, and now, I have cancer. I've done nothing wrong. Why is God punishing me?" Or it could be something like this statement, which contains anger rather than confusion, "To Hell with God. What's the point in believing in God and prayer and then nothing works when you're in trouble? Why is God doing this to my family!?"

In my experience, the "Why God?" question is usually expressed as a statement with confusion or anger. It's interesting that nowhere in the New Testament does Our Lord promise a trouble-free life to His followers, instead, He asks us to take up our cross and follow Him. Yet, many believers have this idea in the 'back of their minds' that *if* I'm good, then good things will happen. So, when all of a sudden, a child gets seriously sick, or a terminal diagnosis follows a long-awaited retirement, then one can be forgiven if they raise their eyes to heaven and says, "What gives?"

It's so important to realise that the "Why God" question is not a request for a theological answer, i.e. "Well, beginning in Genesis we see the Fall of Man, which introduced death and disease into our world and...." Again, like a fix or solution, this is not helpful. People who ask this question are venting. They are going through something so powerful, that it is shaking even their faith in God, and so they are confused or angry about what's happening. When I first started in chaplaincy, this was the question I dreaded, because the truth is, I don't know why God is doing A, B, C, in your life. I have this picture of this loving God, and then in the face of your lived experience, your story, I can struggle to see where God fits in.

As His representative in the hospital, we as chaplains can take the brunt of people's anger about how they feel God has let them down or how heaven appears deaf to their plight. It's so easy to be a fair- weather friend of God, but as soon as dark clouds appear, we start to question everything we believed so easily before. I think this is just a sign of our relative immaturity in the faith, in that we expect good things for being so called good followers, whatever that means. However, it is a very understandable attitude, and one to which I have been guilty of myself. It reminds me of a story from the life of one of the greatest saints in the Roman Catholic Church, St. Teresa of Avila. From the Life of St. Teresa, a 1912 translation by Alice Lady Lovat "taken from the French of 'A Carmelite' Nun," which gives the following story on page 548. In January of the last year of her life, 1582, she left Ávila to establish convents in Burgos and Grenada, and this befell her along the way:

Teresa describes the journey thus: "We had to run many dangers. At no part of the road were the risks greater than within a few leagues of Burgos, at a place called Los Pontes. The rivers were so high that the water in places covered everything, neither road nor the smallest footpath could be seen, only water everywhere, and two abysses on each side. It seemed foolhardiness to advance, especially in a carriage, for if one strayed ever so little off the road (then invisible), one must have perished." The saint is silent on her share of the adventure, but her companions relate that, seeing their alarm, she turned to them and encouraged them, saying that "as they were engaged in doing God's work, how could they die in a better cause?" She then led the way on foot. The current was so strong that she lost her footing and was on the point of being carried away when our Lord sustained her. "Oh, my Lord!" she exclaimed, with her usual loving familiarity, "when wilt Thou cease from scattering obstacles in our path?" "Do not complain, daughter," the Divine Master answered, "for it is ever thus that I treat My friends." "*Ah, Lord, it is also on that account that Thou hast so few!*" was her reply.

As a hospital chaplain, listening to countless tails of sorrow and woe, I find it difficult to argue with the Saint. There have been such horrible stories I have heard, that I have at times prayed to the Lord, "Dear Lord, I know I don't know anymore than a child, maybe even a baby, but the way it looks to me, is that You have been picking on that person,, and they need a break".

I will provide two simple responses to the "Why God?" question which will serve you well:

(1) P: All my life I have been a faithful follower of the Lord, and now, I have cancer. I've done nothing wrong. Why is God punishing me?"

C: It sounds like you're really struggling to make sense of what God's doing in your life".

(2) P: "To Hell with God. What's the point in believing in God and prayer and then nothing works when you're in trouble? Why is God doing this to my family!?"

C: It sounds like you're furious with God at the moment.

Some sort of variation of those responses, allows the person to vent their feelings, and share how what they are going through challenges their faith. In so doing, very often the person will come to certain realisations about their faith and what they believe to be true, and how in some cases these beliefs need updating or dumping. For example, after a period of venting, a person may say, "You know, I don't think I'm angry with God, it's just I'm scared about what the future may bring". This can lead to a conversation in which a person's anxieties/fears/concerns etc can be shared. I always recall that God does not need me to defend Him, and He is not put off by the fears and anger of His children in crisis.

Chapter Thirteen

The Drama Triangle

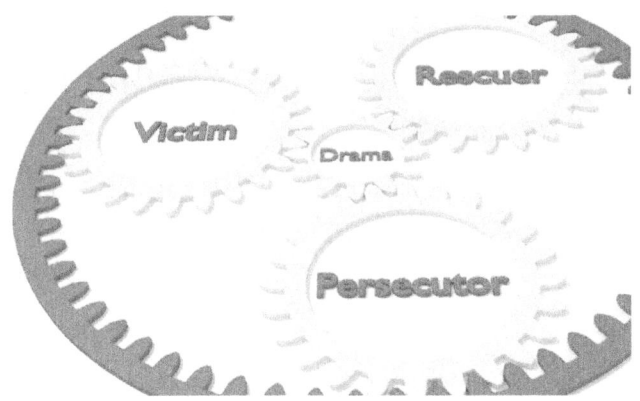

All chaplains must be aware of falling into the dreaded drama triangle. In the late 1960s psychiatrist Stephen Karman described what he called the drama triangle. The triangle represents a dysfunctional personal relationship and illustrates three roles that an individual can play in that relationship: victim, rescuer and persecutor. The roles are not the people themselves, but parts to be played in the drama that occurs as the relationship unfolds. A central role in this drama is that of the victim. The victim feels incapable and powerless. A victim believes that other people or events are acting upon him and there is nothing that he can do about it. Victims often feel mistreated, disadvantaged and sorry for themselves. They take no responsibility for their situation. To the extent a person remains in the victim role, it blocks him from analysing the problem, making decisions and taking action to improve his situation.

Every victim requires a persecutor — something or someone that can be blamed for the victim's situation. A persecutor isn't necessarily always a person; it may be a condition or circumstance the victim perceives as the cause of his woes.

The third role is rescuer — the one who intervenes between the persecutor and victim. He is the person who steps in and says, "I can help; just do what I say and everything will be fine." The person who assumes the role of rescuer does so with a sincere intention to help, but in doing so, perpetuates the victim's feelings of helplessness, reinforces a "poor me" attitude, and either consciously or unconsciously makes the victim dependent upon him. Rescuing others can be addictive. It makes one feel needed, important and in charge. Sometimes it fills a psychological need such that one feels guilty if he doesn't rescue.

There is a legitimate place for these roles. The position of Victim is legitimate when a child is a victim of child abuse. When an adult intervenes to assist a child, he or she serves as a legitimate Rescuer from abuse for the child. The Persecutor position is legitimate when someone sets required limits on abusive behavior or enforces rules that protect the larger community.

However, when we are unintentionally caught in the roles of the drama triangle, this can result in us being caught in a role so much so that Good Listening can be Severely Compromised Because we unwittingly Take Sides and lose Our Objectivity and thus become pastorally ineffective.

<u>The Drama Triangle is in nearly every situation.</u>

When we get caught in the drama triangle, usually we are more reactive, at times we can overreact and take sides. We take sides and begin to see things exclusively through the eyes of one perspective against another. Sometimes this creates an adversarial relationship. In our desire to be helpful, we exaggerate the helplessness of an identified victim but deny our own helplessness. We overlook and minimize the person's capabilities and achievements, feeling more competent in the face of their overstated incompetence. We may lose our concern and understanding for the identified persecutor and overlook our own irritation with the person who has assumed the role of victim. In other words, we can lose our objectivity because we have been emotionally triangulated.

When we take on the Role of The Victim.

We feel exploited and injured by others who we see as having so much more power or authority or capability than we have.

Victims feel hopeless, helpless, overwhelmed, angry and worthless.

Victims feel that people are always going to take advantage of them and that the power to effect change is beyond them.

Victims usually give up, under-function and shut down.

Victims can't take initiative because they don't see that there are any real decisions that are theirs to make.

Victims feel that they are entitled to sympathy, attention and assistance. Others are supposed to take care of them or at least support them. They refuse responsibility for their own motivation and self-direction. Dependency and passivity are exaggerated for Victims.

Role of Persecutor.

We feel justified to become aggressive, attacking and punitive. We are obviously the only ones who can get things done around here. We may punish by active aggression or by hostile withholding and huffy withdrawal. Sometimes, we move to this role after we have over functioned as Rescuer. We resent the burden of taking care of others even when we initiate the actions.

The following example, which illustrates how easy it is for a chaplain to find themselves in the drama triangle between a patient and staff, comes from a selected extract of Cathy Hasty's article: "Using a Modification of the Classic Drama Triangle to Enhance Pastoral Care."

(*Journal of Pastoral Care,* Summer 2001, Vol.55, No.2 p 147-157)

Clinical Example: Dr. Lee is a Physician to Mr. Allen and a member of the Liver Transplant Selection Committee. Mr. Allen is a potential candidate for a liver transplant. Chaplain Rowe is the Chaplain on the Transplant Team.

Dr. Lee ends an intense confrontation of Mr. Allen concerning diet, alcohol consumption, medication and lifestyle with this proclamation.

"Mr. Allen, you have been non-compliant and irresponsible concerning your medical treatment. I am not able to recommend you to the Selection Committee (for a liver transplant) because of your current alcohol abuse and your inability to follow instructions. You will need to be substance free for a year before we will re-evaluate you for this transplant. I am sick and tired of seeing you kill yourself."

The next day, the tearful patient, describes that interaction to Chaplain Rowe:

Mr. Allen: Dr Mitchell was very cruel to me. I try very hard but I have a language problem. I did not understand all of the medical language. And I just go off the diet a little and I am hardly drinking anything these days. I am doing the best I can. I will die without that liver. Isn't there something someone can do to help me? Can't you make him to reconsider? Can I get another one of the doctors to recommend me?"

On day three, Chaplain Rowe attends the Liver Transplant Selection Committee with the surgeons, hematologists, nurses, transplant coordinators, and the social worker.

When Mr. Allen is presented by Dr. Lee, **Chaplain Rowe** says:

"Dr. Lee, Mr. Allen reported that you were cruel with him, telling him that he was not getting a transplant and that you were sick of him. I think you should reconsider. He says he is not drinking much and can stop. He has many problems and he will get so sick, and maybe even die, over the next year without that transplant. He wants another physician who can be more objective."

Dr Lee to Chaplain Smith:

"The team and I have invested a great deal in Mr. Allen. We have taken care of him for much longer than you have. We are at the end of the rope. Since he will not comply with the medications, the recovery program or the diet, he will end up rejecting the transplant and needing another, ruining everything I work so hard to do. These are complex and difficult medical decisions that we have to take. There is nothing I can do to help him when he won't stop drinking".

On day four, the doctor tells Mr. Allen that the chaplain suggested Mr. Allen wanted a new doctor. Dr Lee says that Mr. Allen is welcome to see if he can get a new doctor.

Mr. Allen says, "Oh, Doctor, you have been so good to me. I would never think about changing to anyone else. Please don't turn me over to anyone else's care. You know what is best."

Later, on day four, **Mr. Allen says to Chaplain Rowe**: "You don't have any right to say anything bad about my doctor. He is a good person who knows so much. I don't want you coming back to see me if you are going to interfere with his work."

Chaplain Rowe responds to Mr. Allen: "I was only trying to help you and do what you said you wanted. It was difficult too for me to bring this up with the doctor. Maybe I need to get someone else to work with you."

On day five, when Mr. Allen reports to Dr Lee that he told the chaplain off. Dr Lee says "The chaplain was only doing what he thought was right.I want you to continue to see the chaplain. He is a valuable part of the team and has been important to you during this illness."

Chaplain Rowe responds "I don't think that I have any more to offer to this patient. I have other patients and families where I can invest my time."

A modification of the Drama Triangle might have offered the pastoral caregiver more creative and life-giving options in this and other clinical situations. Without reflection the participants avoided their underlying, often unconscious anxiety, shame, anger and hopelessness by blaming others, over functioning or withdrawing in despair. Nothing constructive or redemptive occurred.

It is clear that Chaplain Rowe was emotionally caught in the Drama triangle and persecuted Dr Lee, for example, see his response, "Dr Lee, Mr. Allen reported to me that you were very cruel to him, telling him that he was very unlikely to get the liver transplant and that you were fed up with his negative attitude. I really think you should not be so hasty and reconsider and these are the reasons." Perhaps Chaplain Rowe should be aware of being triangulated and instead of reacting or even overreacting by persecuting Dr Lee, Chaplain Rowe should listen more carefully to the feelings of Mr. Allen and reflect back to Mr. Allen what he may be feeling about Dr Lee.

Look again at what Mr. Allen said to the chaplain, "Chaplain Rowe, yesterday Dr Lee was very cruel to me. He accused me of not trying hard enough! I try very hard but he is not satisfied and my English is not as good as his. I did not understand all the medical words he used but I could see that he was angry with me. He accused me of not trying hard enough and he told me that I may not get on the program. Chaplain, you have got to talk to him. I will die if I don't get a liver transplant."

A more appropriate response to Mr. Allen might have been, "Mr. Allen, you sound very upset with Dr Lee for not believing you and you feel that was very unfair. You desperately want me to try and change his mind about you otherwise you are scared that you will die if you don't get a liver transplant. I am not so sure that I can change his mind, but, what I will do, is to ask him what are your chances of getting a liver transplant".

If Chaplain Rowe did speak to Dr Lee, he could have asked in a private capacity but not in a committee meeting. "Dr Lee, I am wondering whether I could ask you about Mr. Allen's case. What do you think are his chances of getting a liver transplant?"

Notice that the approach is non–persecutory and there is no finger pointing and no taking of sides. This approach allows Dr Lee to be non-defensive and to ventilate any frustrations that he may have about Mr. Allen.

Strategy to Follow: Check List: Am I taking sides?

If so, you may very likely be caught in a drama triangle. Try not to react, but wait, and reflect and respond with empathy. Step out of the Triangle and listen carefully to the feelings of the person who may want you to take their side and reflect what they may be feeling, for e.g., you sound very frustrated, angry, upset, annoyed, helpless etc. For example, "You seem to feel that he is not listening, that you are not making any progress in your …etc.".

So, what's the solution: Don't get trapped in the drama triangle to begin with. However, that is often easier said than done. Here are some guidelines to help avoid the trap:

1. Become aware of when a drama triangle is present. Look for its symptoms as you watch others interact, or as you interact with them. Awareness is 80 percent of the answer. Learn to recognise a rescue while you are doing it. When you can see it, you can avoid it.

2. When you observe someone playing the victim role, treat them as an adult. Adults are responsible for their own lives. Adults can figure out what to do, how to solve their own problems and take action, albeit with some real help from time to time. If someone is playing the role of victim, don't buy it.

3. Empower, don't rescue. As a chaplain, you are not a saviour. Your role is not to solve anyone's problem. However, you are expected to help others by using the pastoral conversation, in order for people to find their own solutions and resources.

Chapter Fourteen

Pastoral Prayer

Mary Oliver's (1992) lines from The Summer Day:

I don't know exactly what a prayer is.

I do know how to pay attention, how to fall down

into the grass, how to kneel down in the grass,

how to be idle and blessed, how to stroll through the fields,

which is what I have been doing all day.

Tell me, what else should I have done?

Doesn't everything die at last, and too soon?

Tell me, what is it you plan to do with your one wild and precious life?

I started this book telling you that there were two main types of conversations we are involved in as chaplains, well there are also different types of prayer. The tendency to embrace prayer in times of fear and neediness is a human and almost universal one. It is a form of expressing hope. Everyone prays, and it would be difficult to find a person who in one crisis or another lifted their eyes to the heavens with a cry for help. With prayer there is personal prayer, corporate prayer and pastoral prayer. Pastoral prayer runs to the same rules as a pastoral conversation, it is completely focused on the other person's revealed needs. They again set the agenda.

Therefore, we need to be aware of our motivation to pray. It is very easy for prayer to become another way for us to try and fix the suffering rather than be comfortable with them and listening. Kelcourse (2001) states:

Prayer is more than a bowed head and folded hands. It begins with the deepest longings of our hearts, as expressed by our mute bodies, with sighs too deep for words. Chaplains who are not afraid of their own pain, their own dark voids, can risk the attention required to meet another, soul to soul, through the dialogues and rituals that healing transformation requires. Suffering not engaged robs life of meaning. Suffering deliberately faced, through the dialogues of the soul in prayer, makes us co-creators with God. Like Wisdom herself, we hover over the primordial face of the deep, trusting that creation, and the light it brings, will be good.

Three things help us not only listen pastorally but also pray pastorally.

1. We don't have to pray with the person groaning for God to hear us

If we have had a conversation with someone that has not mentioned God but has shared a significant loss with us, it can seem normal to us to offer prayer. Sure, our motivation is right, we want to intercede on their behalf and petition God to act but do we think that God listens more if we say the prayer out loud with the person or can we trust that He will listen just as well if we pray after we have left?

We can have a sense that we have been more helpful to someone if we have prayed with them. However, if they have not mentioned God, nor asked for prayer and we offer to pray, they can sometimes think that we only listened so that we could get our God stuff in. When we listen well and wait to clarify *their choice* about prayer, it then will mean a great deal to them.

2. Let the person groaning set the agenda by CLARIFY CHOICES

It is important that we clarify choices when someone asks for prayer. We need to ask, "Would they be comfortable if I prayed aloud here?" and "What would they specifically like me to mention in the prayer?" If we are sitting in a public place and the person is not comfortable with us praying aloud, then what comfort does the prayer bring, it becomes more about us satisfying our need to do something.

3. If we pray make sure the content is set by the person groaning

We need to contain all our normal prayer language and pray simple clear prayers that reflect only what the person has told us. We have to be careful not to problem solve the issues with God making suggestions about how He might intervene. Sometimes without noticing we can use prayer to make judgments or give advice to the person. If we do this our prayer has become another way of us falling into the trap of being a "quick speaker" when what we want is to be a "quick listener". So not only do we want our responses to be full of empathy, but we want our prayers to be full of empathy as well. To pray with someone is a great privilege but let us do it in such a way that it is full of respect, trusting that our God is listening and involved in everything.

At first, the thought of being called by a family in the Emergency Department for a spontaneous prayer filled me with dread. That may surprise some, but for me, praying aloud for people was not a normal part of my spiritual life. What I learnt to do, was when I attended such a situation, and typically the family was present, rather than read out some prayer that I knew or I had downloaded off the internet, I asked the family members, for example, "What can you tell me about your mum?" I would listen to the things they told me: they were a loving mother and grandmother; a devoted wife; very active in her Church/community; great sense of humour etc. etc. I would then say a prayer incorporating these attributes, and this made the prayer feel more natural and personal.

Scenario Discussion Exercises - Possible Responses

Pat

1. I think Pat is not going to have any sense that he has been heard & understood because the reply is both a piece of advice & a correction to Pat's perspective especially about the doctor. Pat has asked for neither. They are 'fix it ' statements.

2. His expectation that his health would be OK has been shattered. It would not be unusual for Pat to have a sense that his life he was hoping to have has been ripped away from him. One could imagine that if Pat continued to groan all of the basic loss types would be mentioned.

3. I think anger is the emotion most clearly expressed. I would not be surprised for Pat also to feel very sad & very scared. These emotions may have been expressed if Pat continued to groan.

4. Possible Response - "Oh, no – it sounds just so infuriating! You thought the doctor was going give all the clear but it's the opposite."

Susanne

1. I would not be surprised if Suzi was thinking to herself 'why did I bother opening my mouth. I have just been told that what was so important to me was really nothing at all.' The response looks like a very clear effort change Susi's perspective. Suzi is not asking for this but rather hoping that someone might value her & what she is going through.

2. It would seem that Suzi is mentioning relational losses to do with her boyfriend (the break-up) & her mum (keeps asking rather than listening). Possibly an identity loss as well (only one without partner).

3. Again, I think anger is the emotion most clearly expressed. If groan continued sadness may be expressed over loss of relationship and/or scared about an uncertain future regarding relationships.

4. Possible Response - "Sounds frustrating, your Mum doesn't seem to be listening to you."

Brett

1. Bret will not want to keep on speaking. He has a sense that his parents don't care about his wishes & now that theme continues with the listener not caring about his feelings or his perspective as all they want to do is defend the parents.

2. Not only has Bret lost his brother he has lost the opportunity to be at the scattering of his ashes. Also, his parents have possibly treated him like a child by not telling him about the scattering therefore making his choice for him.

3. Again anger. Again, if groan continued sadness may be expressed over loss of brother and/or scared that his parents may have the perception that he would not care or make the time for his brother's ashes ceremony.

4. Possible Response - "That sounds so annoying, you missed the scattering of your brother's ashes."

Reference List

Autton, N. (1986). *Pain: An Exploration*. London: Darton, Longman and Todd.

Benson, H., & Stark, M. (1996). *Timeless healing: The power and biology of belief*. New York: Fireside

Berkowitz, M. R. (2018). 'Standing in their shoes - Kashouvot has introduced pastoral care as an integral part of the health care provided in hospitals and nursing homes in Israel.', *Jerusalem Post, The: Web Edition Articles (Israel)*, 21 Mar, (online NewsBank).

Bogia, B. P. (1985). Responding to Questions in Pastoral Care. *Journal of Pastoral Care, 39*(4), 357–369. https://doi.org/10.1177/002234098503900407

Baruth, L. G., & Huber, C. H. (1985). *Counseling and psychotherapy: Theoretical analyses and skills applications*. Columbus: Merri.

Boyd, G. E. (2003). "Pastoral Conversation: Relational Listening and Open-Ended Questions". *Pastoral Psychology* 51 (5): 340-60 DOI:10.1023/A:10236140428

Carnegie, D. (1967). *How to Win Friends and Influence People*. Sydney: Angus & Robertson.

Collins, G. R. (1995). *How to be a People Helper: A Christian psychologist shares insights that will help you help your friends, family and co-workers*. Wheaton, Illinois: Tyndale House Publishers.

Dossey, L. (1996). *Prayer is good medicine: How to reap the healing benefits of prayer*. San Francisco: Harper Collins.

Ekman, P. (1985). *Telling Lies: Clues to deceit in the marketplace, politics and marriage*. New York: Norton.

Grundmann, C. H. (2003). To Be With Them: A Hospital Chaplain's Reflection of the Beside Ministry to Terminally Ill and Dying People. *Christian Bioethics: Non-Ecumenical Studies in Medical Morality*, 9(1), 79–90. https://doi-org.rp.nla.gov.au/10.1093/chbi.9.1.79.17379

Kelcourse, F.B. (2001) 'Prayer and the Soul: Dialogues That Heal', *Journal of Religion and Health*, 40(1), pp. 231–241. Available at: https://search.ebscohost.com/login.aspx?direct=true&db=edsjsr&AN=edsjsr.27511519&site=eds-live (Accessed: 28 November 2022).

Kelly, E. (2012). *Personhood and Presence: Self as a resource for spiritual and pastoral care.* New York: Bloomsbury Publishing.

Lawrence E. Holst. (1985) *Hospital Ministry: The Role of the Chaplain Today* New York: Crossroad Publishing.

Meacham, J. (2012). *Thomas Jefferson: The art of power.* New York, NY: The Random House Publishing Company.

Nouwen, Henri J. M (1972) *The Wounded Healer: Ministry in Contemporary Society.* New York:Image Doubleday

Rogers, C. R. (1980). *A Way of Being.* Boston: Houghton Mifflin.

Wells, S. (2017). "Hovering Over the Deep". *Christian Century* 134 (17): 28-31

https://search.ebscohost.com/login.aspx?direct=true&db=a9h&AN=124469485&site=eds-live.

Wuellner, Flora Slosson. (1995). *Prayer, Stress and Our Inner Wounds.* Nashville, Tennessee: The Upper Room.

Zagdanski, D. (1994) *Stuck for Words: What to say to someone who is grieving.* Melbourne, Australia

Printed in Great Britain
by Amazon

62175877R00141